justice
ain't got
no age

BE WARNED AND AWARE

What follows are the accounts
and adventures of young
Boyd Linney, also know as the

COW BOY™

Boyd's exploits ain't for those with weak
bellies and genteel dispositions.
If you ain't sure of your belly or
disposition's fortitude, please consult
your local sawbones before turning
this here page.

COW BOY: A BOY

has been brought to y'all

Fella what goes by Mister

NATE COSBY

came up with the script  story, then

COW BOY'S

comprised of five chapters, broken up by brand-new yarns, courtesy of

Mister ROGER LANGRIDGE

Mister BRIAN CLEVINGER,
Mister SCOTT WEGENER, Mister MITCH GERADS

Ms. COLLEEN COOVER

Mister MIKE MAIHACK.

COW BOY was created by Mister Nate Cosby and Mister Chris Eliopoulos, but it would not have been possible without the aid of Mister CLAYTON COWLES.

AND HIS HORSE ™

by these fine folk...

Mister
CHRIS ELIOPOULOS

came along and drew, colored and lettered it.

This here book's been published by the fine folks at ARCHAIA ENTERTAINMENT LLC

Mister **SCOTT NEWMAN** is the Manager of Production
Mister **PAUL MORRISSEY** is our fine editor
Mister **P.J. BICKETT** is the Chief Executive Officer
Mister **MARK SMYLIE** is the Chief Creative Officer
Mister **MIKE KENNEDY** is Archaia's Publisher
And the handsome Mister **STEPHEN CHRISTY** is the Editor-In-Chief

ARCHAIA ™

Archaia Entertainment LLC
1680 Vine Street, Suite 1010
Los Angeles, California, 90028, USA
www.Archaia.com

COW BOY. March 2012.
FIRST PRINTING
10 9 8 7 6 5 4 3 2 1
ISBN: 1-936393-67-0
ISBN-13: 978-1-936393-67-1

Printed in China by Global PSD.

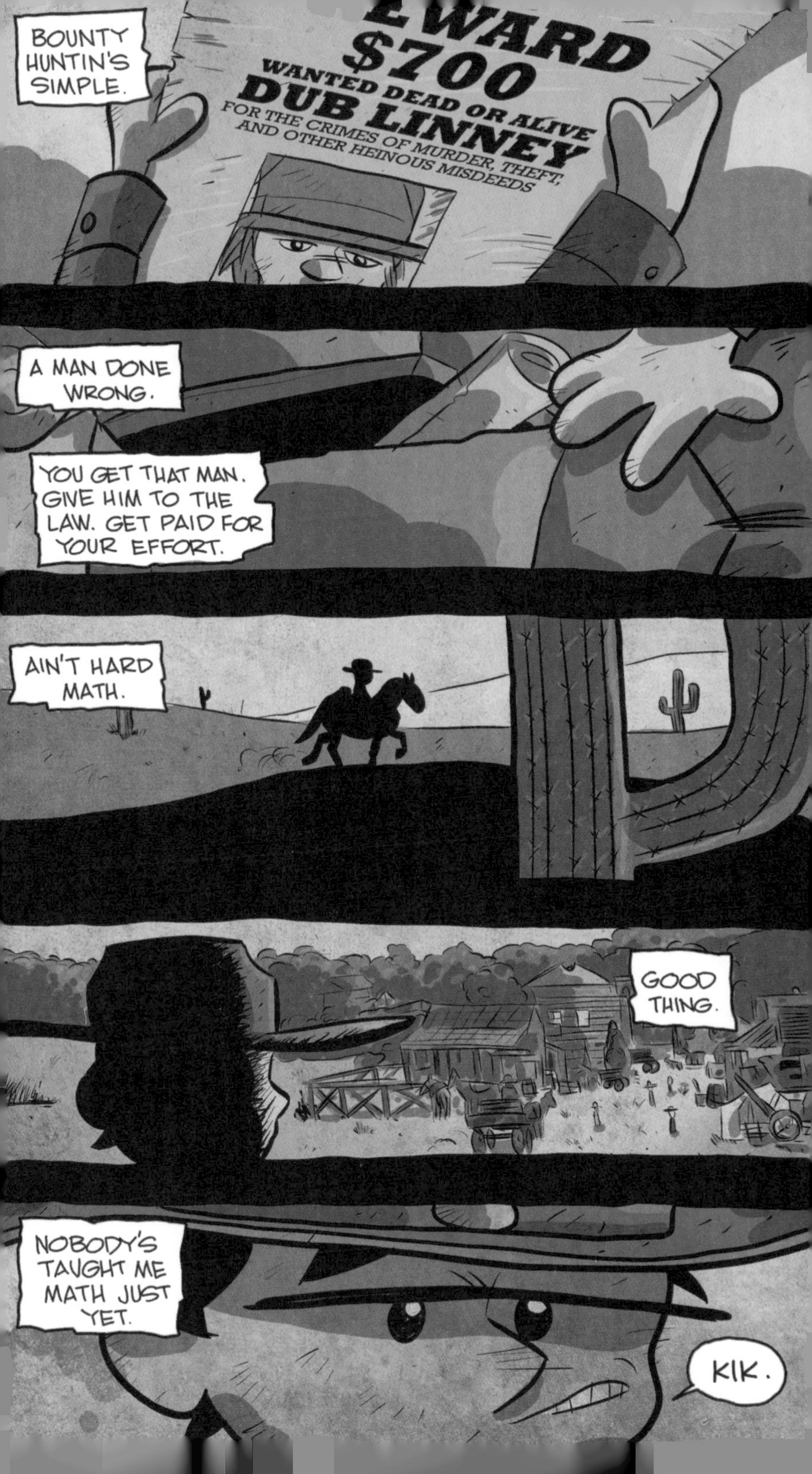
BOUNTY HUNTIN'S SIMPLE.
EWARD
$700
WANTED DEAD OR ALIVE
DUB LINNEY
FOR THE CRIMES OF MURDER, THEFT, AND OTHER HEINOUS MISDEEDS
A MAN DONE WRONG.
YOU GET THAT MAN. GIVE HIM TO THE LAW. GET PAID FOR YOUR EFFORT.
AIN'T HARD MATH.
GOOD THING.
NOBODY'S TAUGHT ME MATH JUST YET.
KIK.

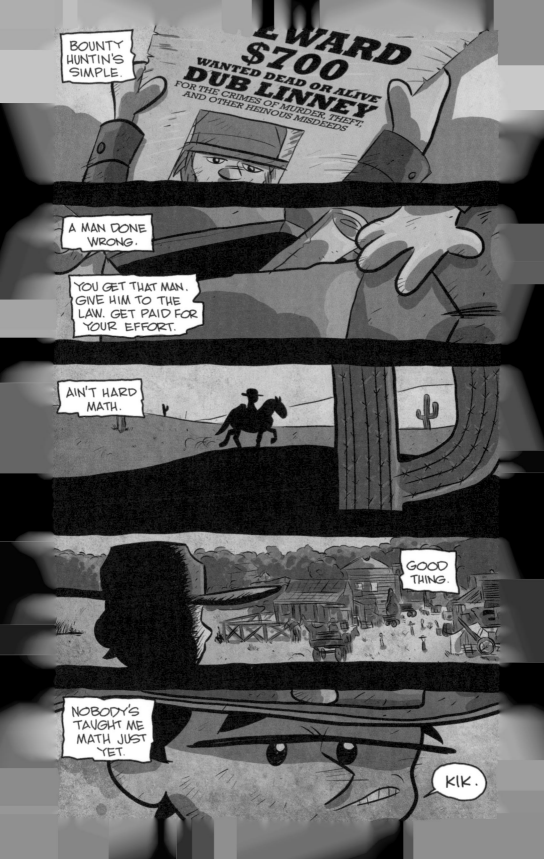

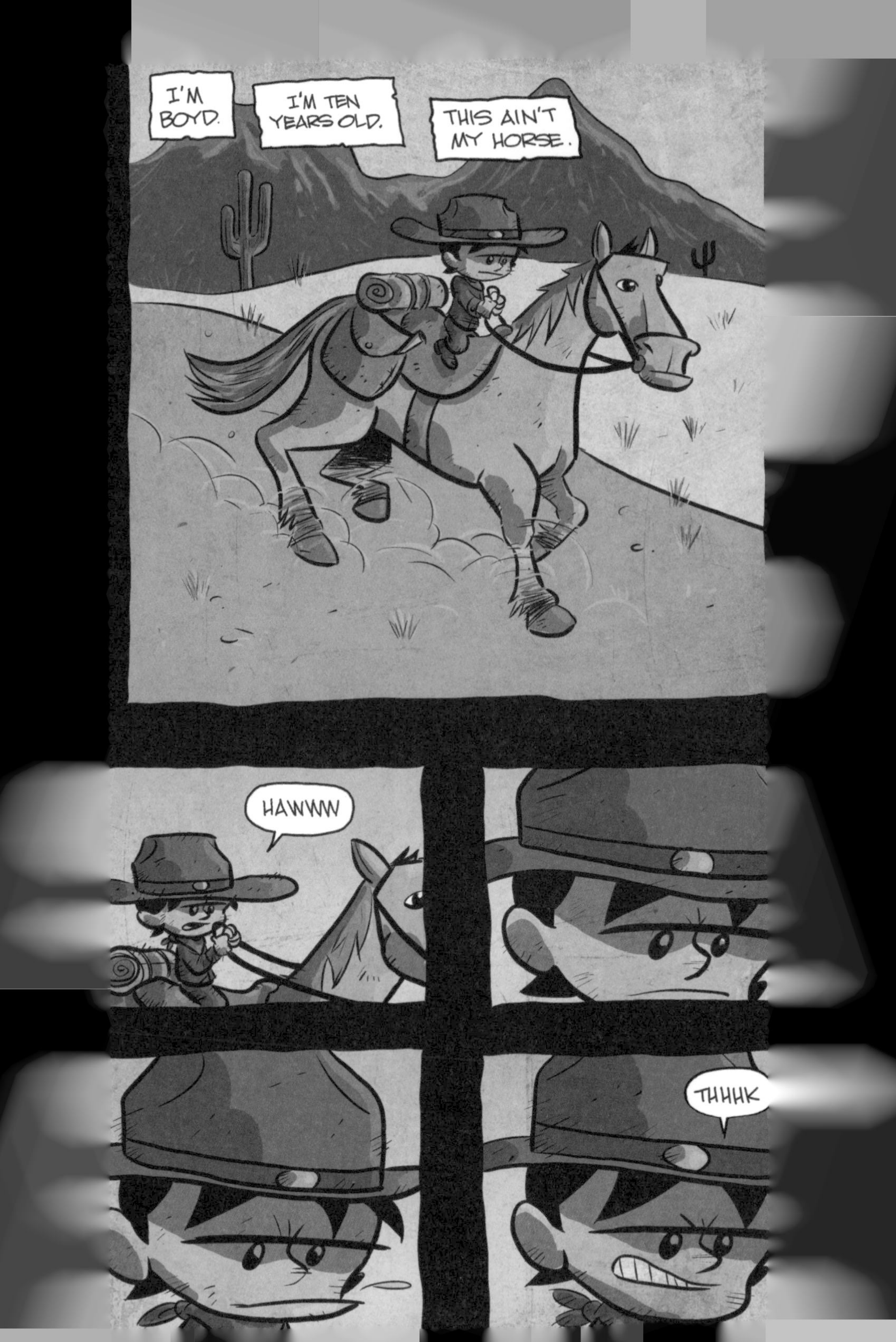
I'M BOYD.
I'M TEN YEARS OLD.
THIS AIN'T MY HORSE.
HAWWW
THHHK

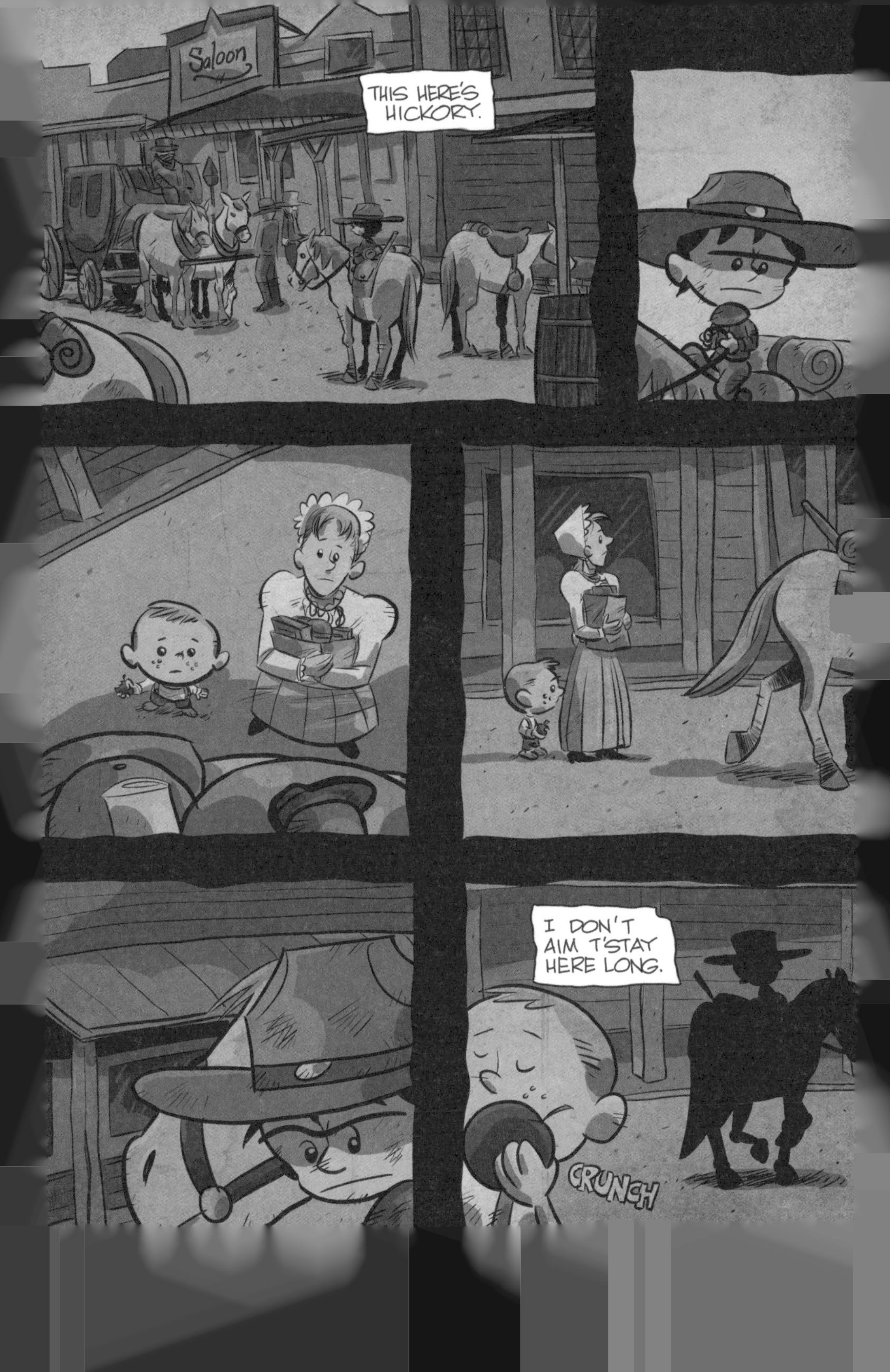
Saloon
THIS HERE'S HICKORY.
I DON'T AIM T'STAY HERE LONG.
CRUNCH

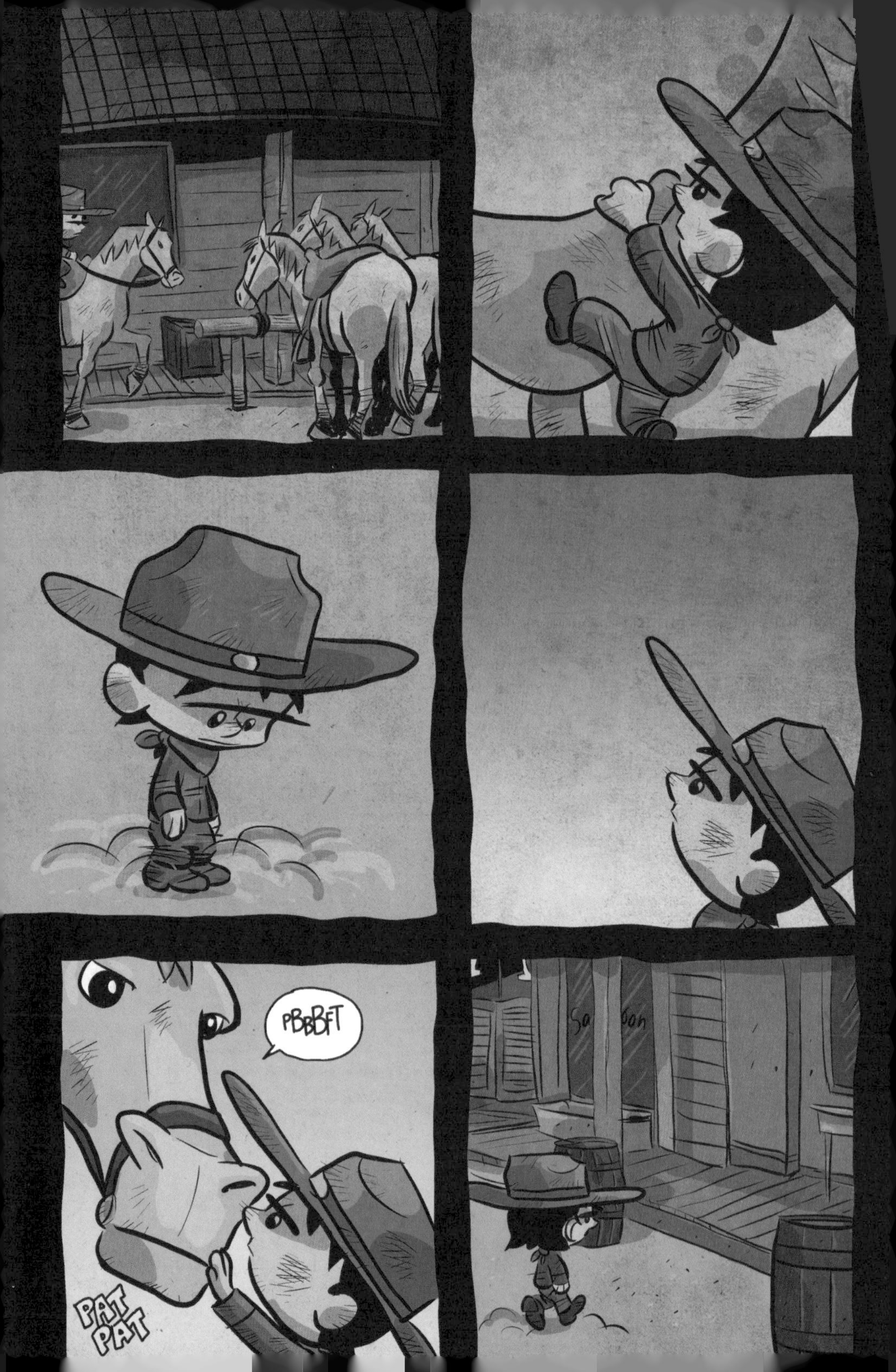
PBBBFT
PAT PAT

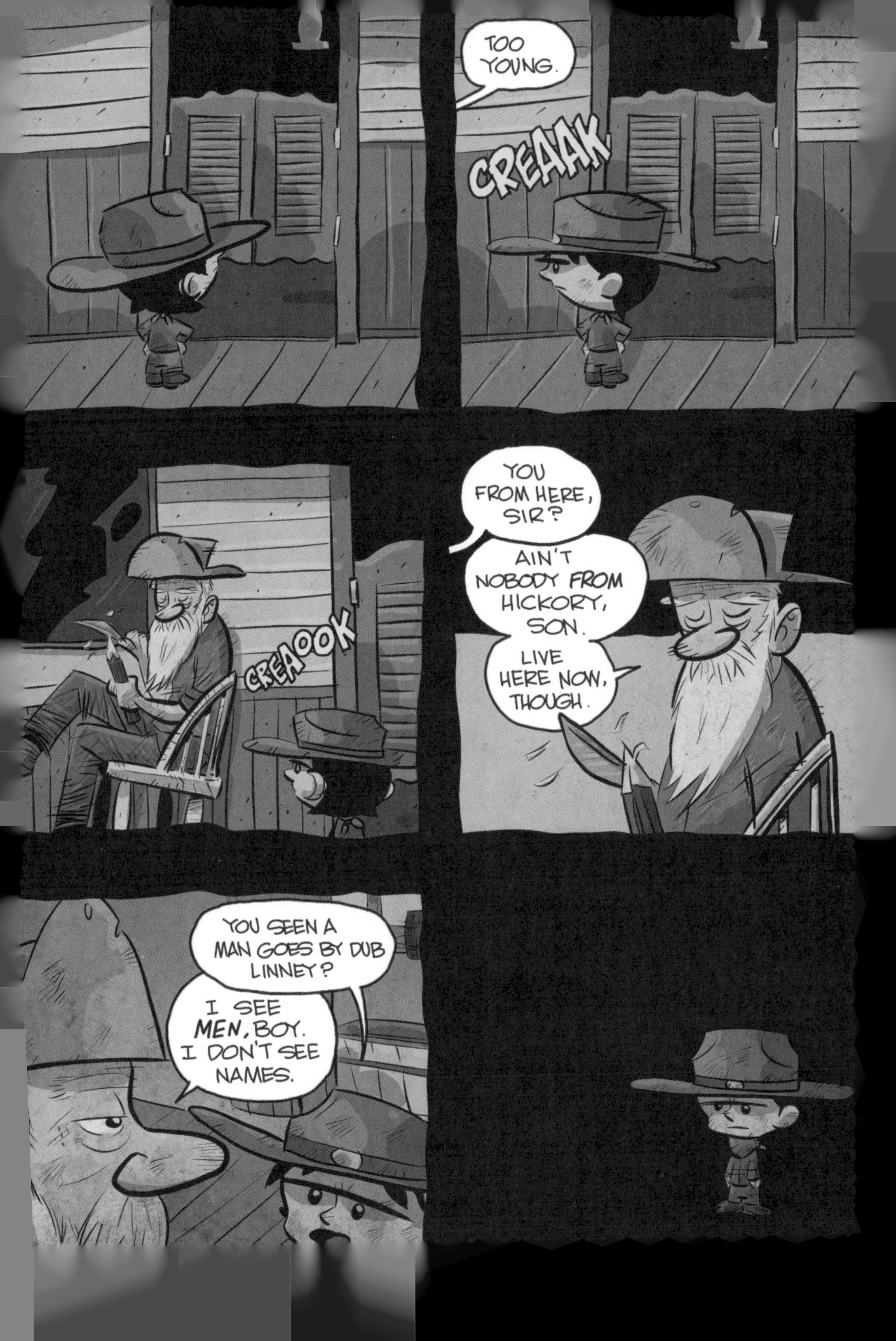
TOO YOUNG.
CREAAK
CREAOOK
YOU FROM HERE, SIR?
AIN'T NOBODY FROM HICKORY, SON.
LIVE HERE NOW, THOUGH.
YOU SEEN A MAN GOES BY DUB LINNEY?
I SEE MEN, BOY. I DON'T SEE NAMES.

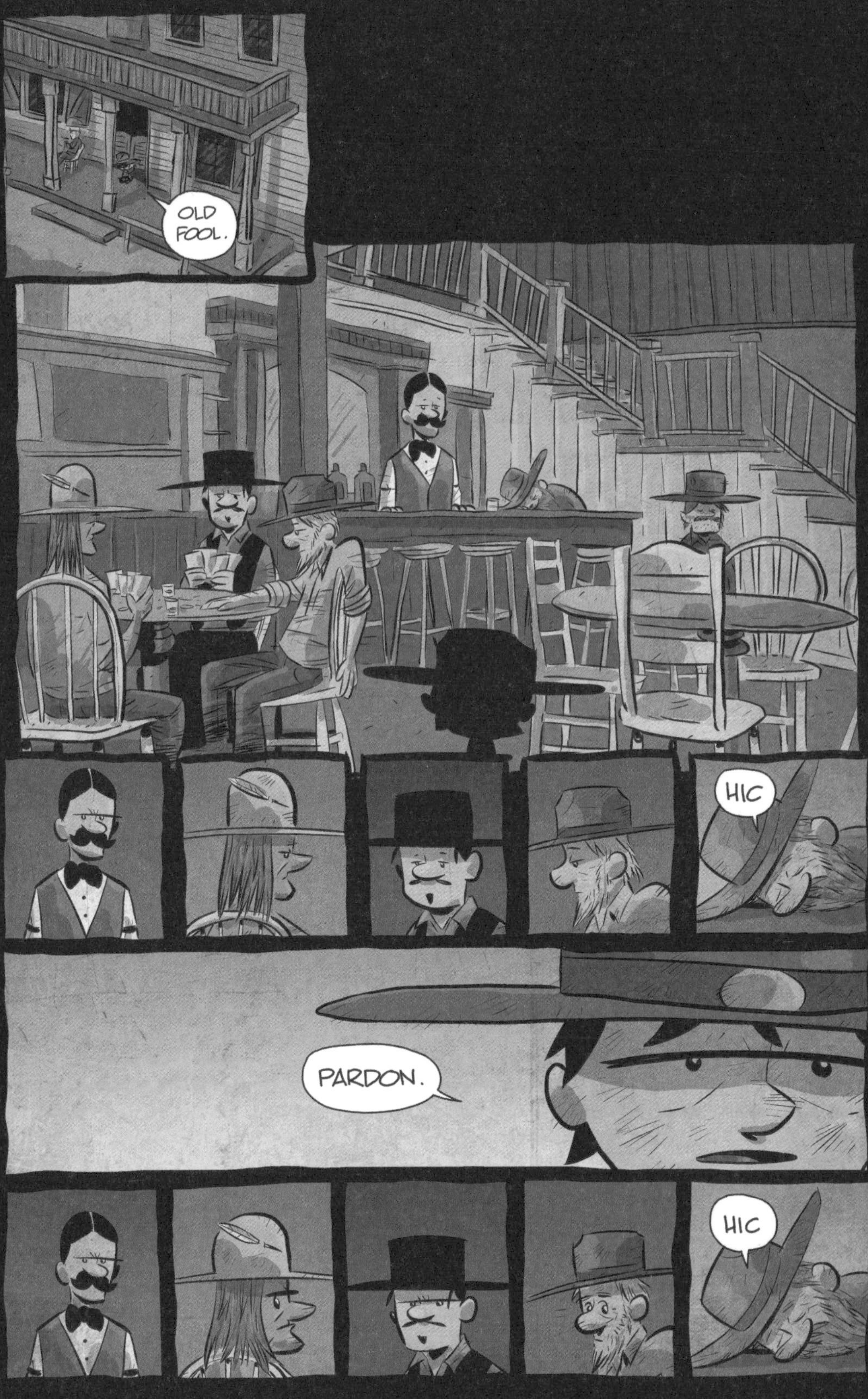
OLD FOOL.
HIC
PARDON.
HIC

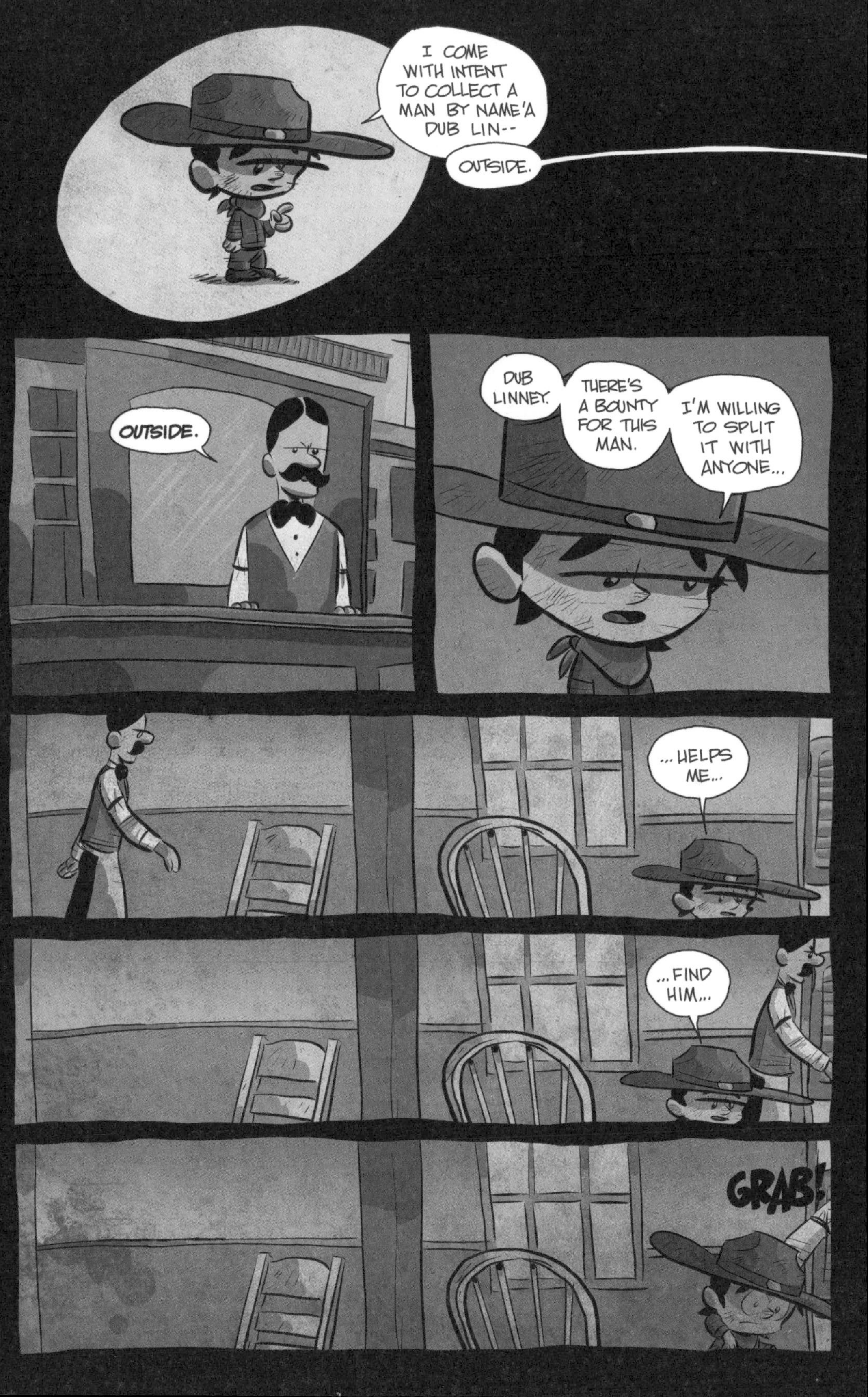
I COME WITH INTENT TO COLLECT A MAN BY NAME'A DUB LIN--
OUTSIDE.
OUTSIDE.
DUB LINNEY.
THERE'S A BOUNTY FOR THIS MAN.
I'M WILLING TO SPLIT IT WITH ANYONE...
...HELPS ME...
...FIND HIM...
GRAB!

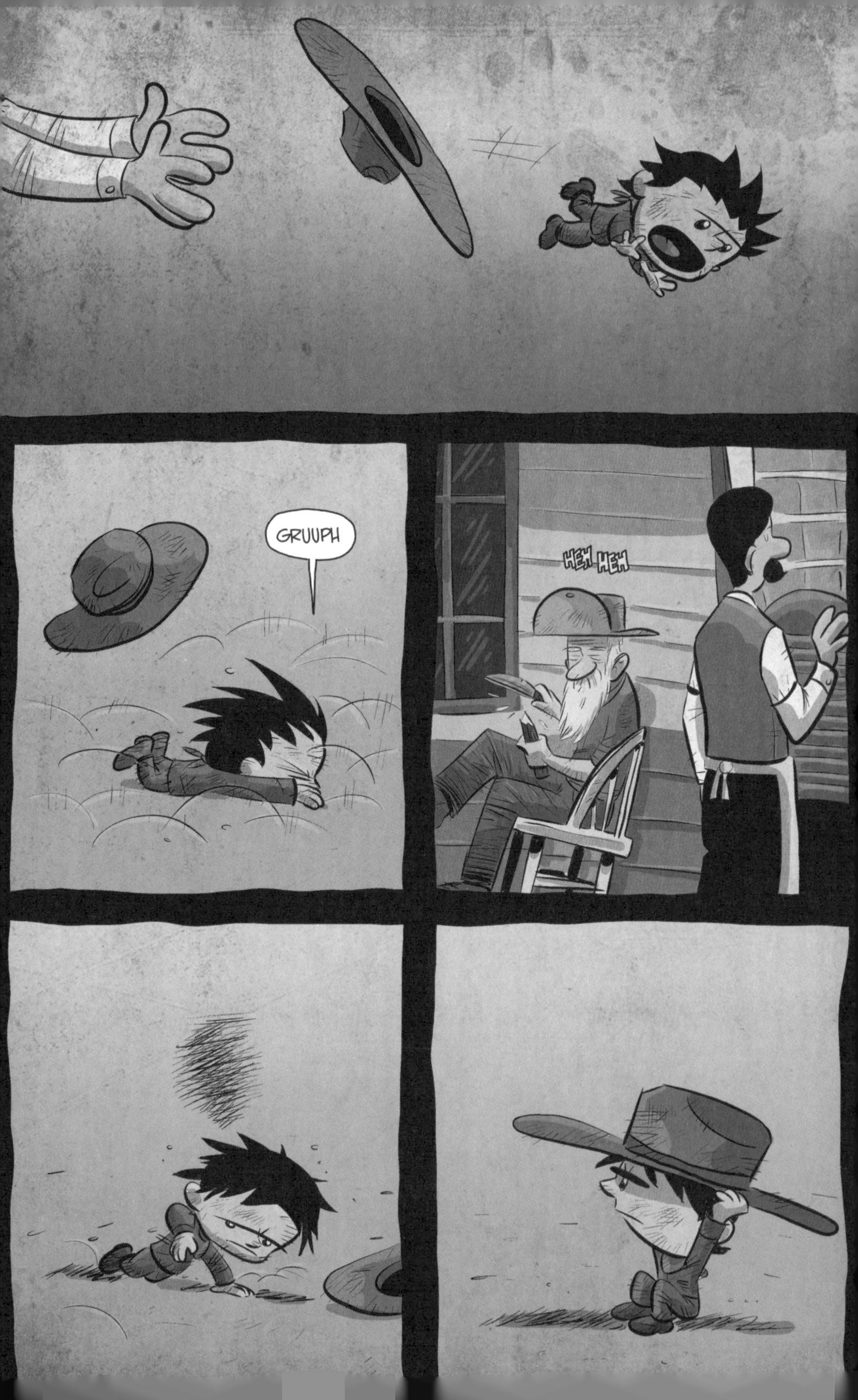
GRUUPH
HEH HEH

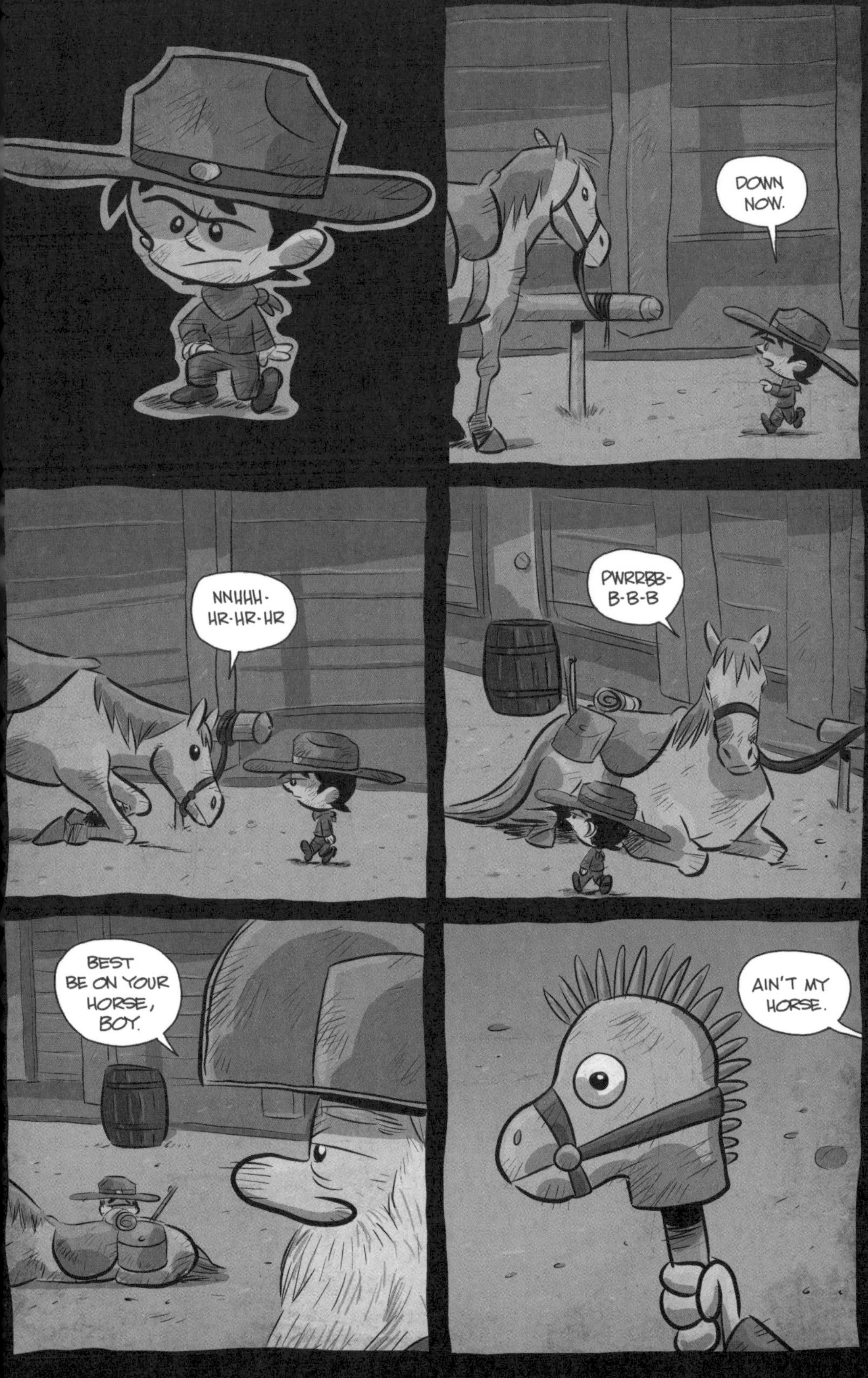
DOWN NOW.
NNHHH-HR-HR-HR
PWRRBB-B-B-B
BEST BE ON YOUR HORSE, BOY.
AIN'T MY HORSE.

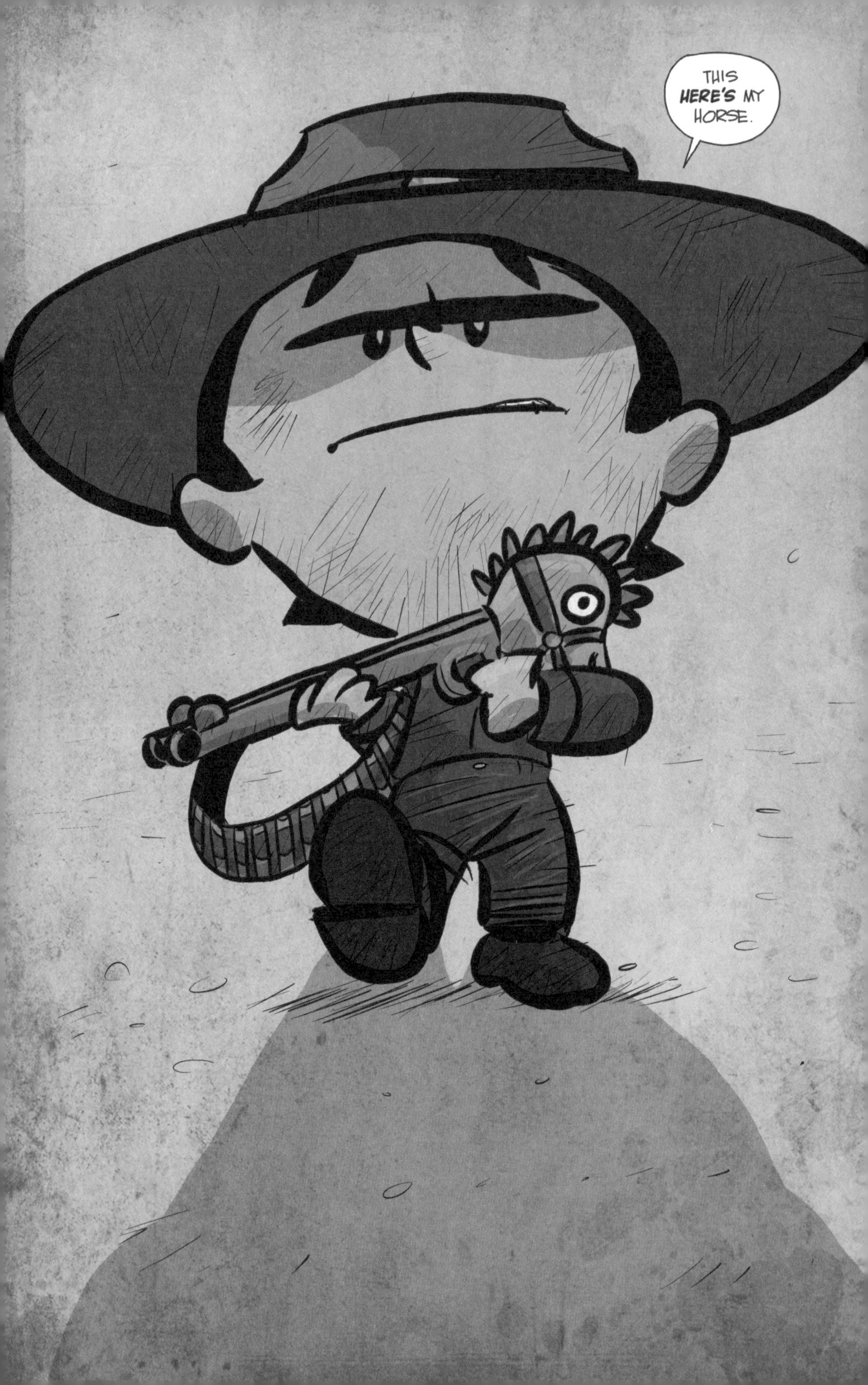
THIS HERE'S MY HORSE.

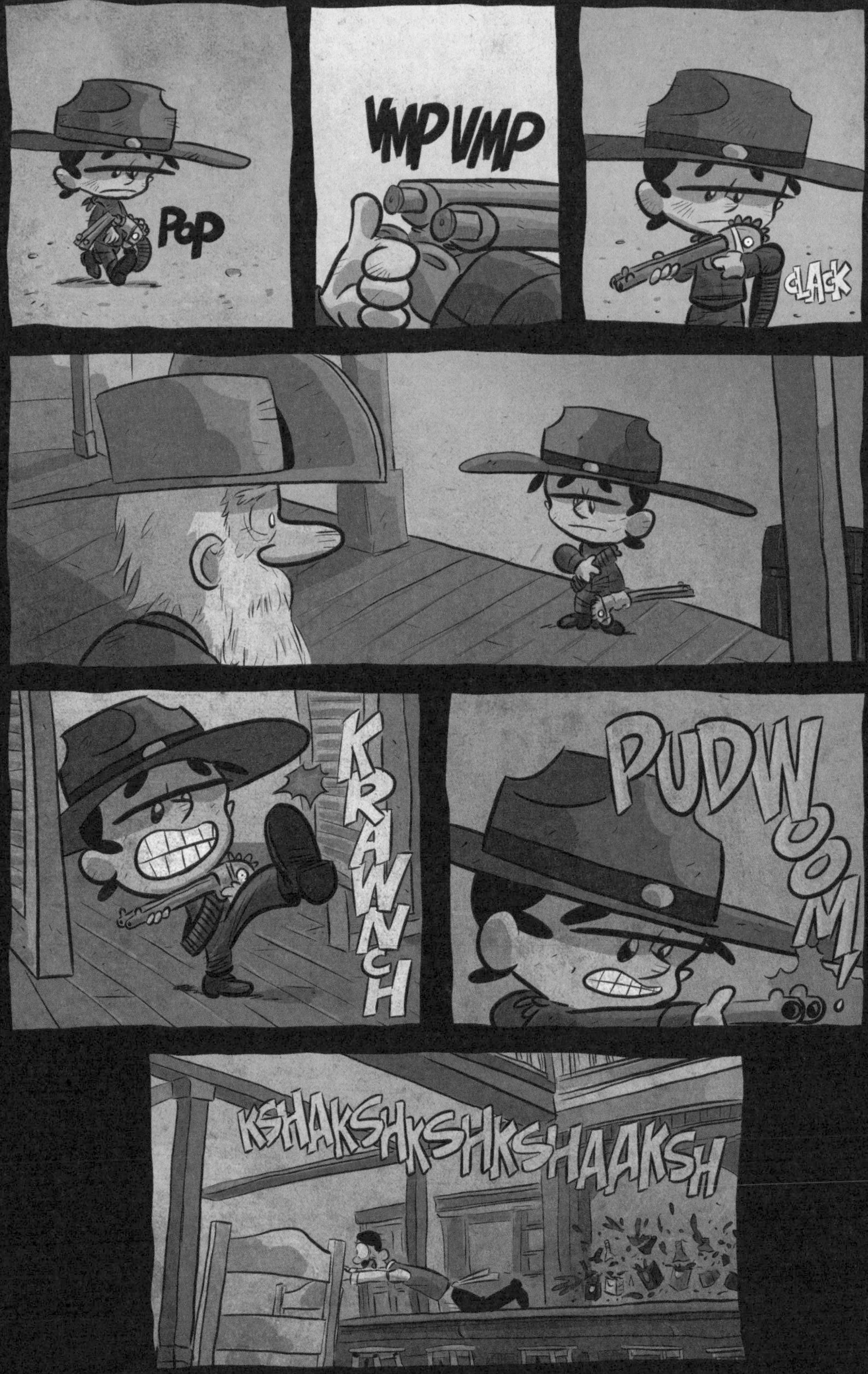
POP
VMP VMP
CLACK
KRAWNCH
PUDWOOOM!
KSHAKSHKSHKSHAAKSH

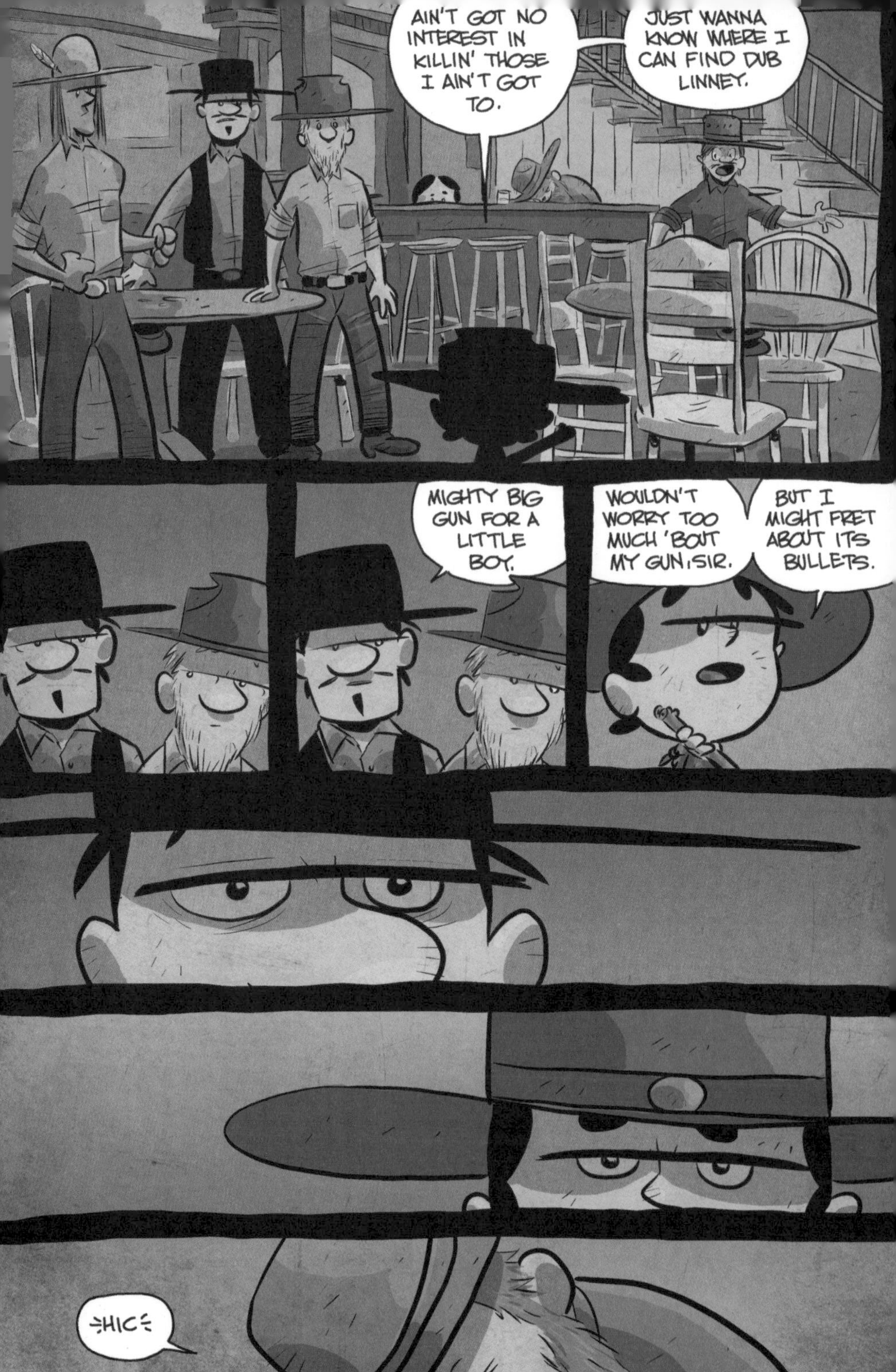
AIN'T GOT NO INTEREST IN KILLIN' THOSE I AIN'T GOT TO.
JUST WANNA KNOW WHERE I CAN FIND DUB LINNEY.
MIGHTY BIG GUN FOR A LITTLE BOY.
WOULDN'T WORRY TOO MUCH 'BOUT MY GUN, SIR.
BUT I MIGHT FRET ABOUT ITS BULLETS.
HIC

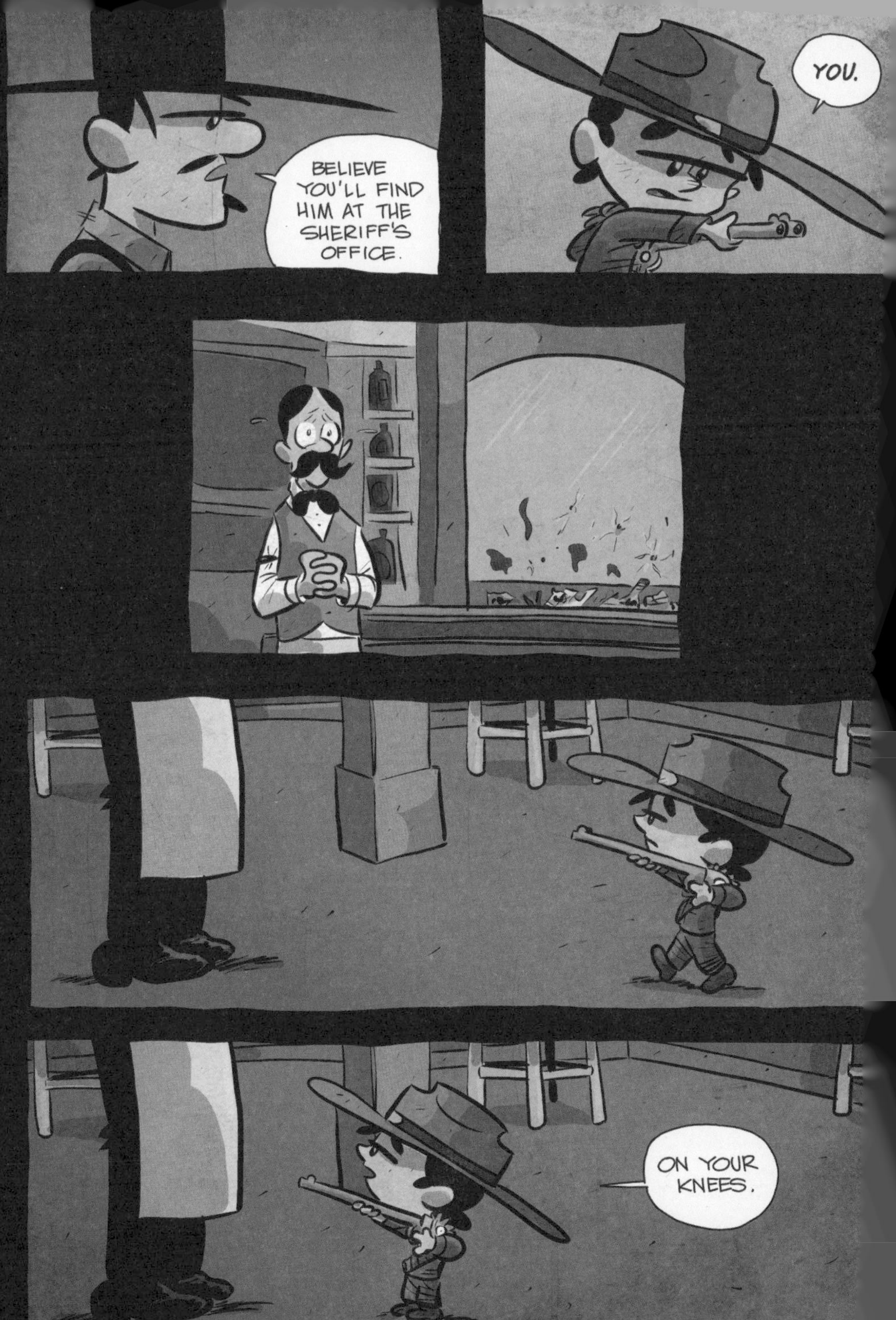
BELIEVE YOU'LL FIND HIM AT THE SHERIFF'S OFFICE.
YOU.
ON YOUR KNEES.

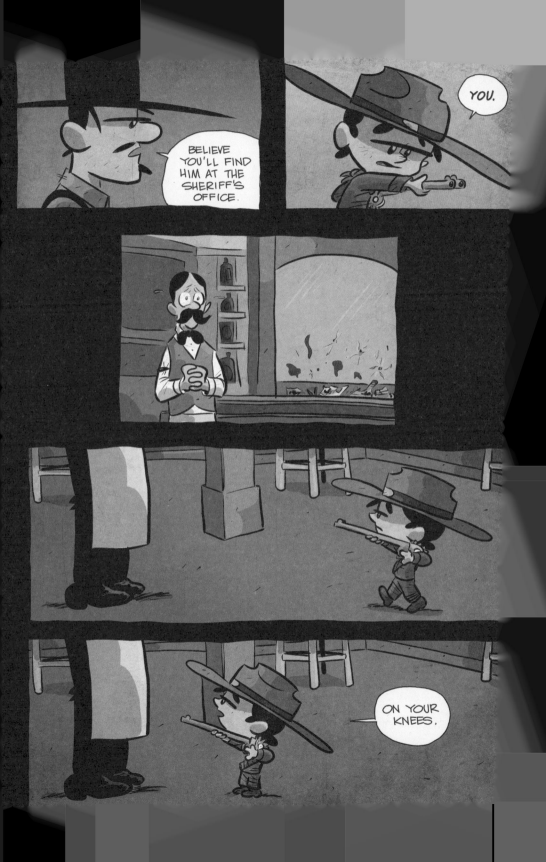

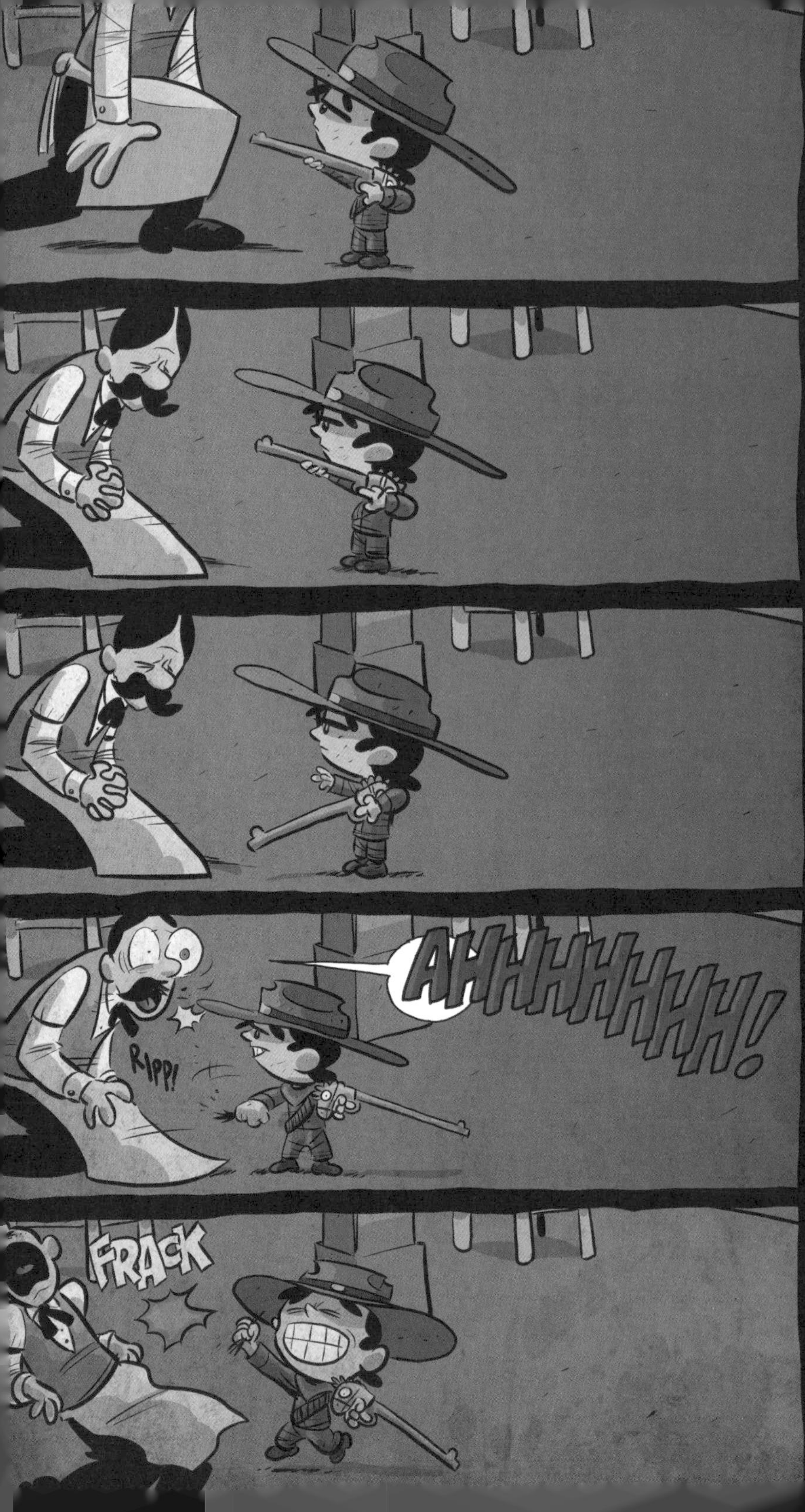
AHHHHHHHH!
RIPP!
FRACK

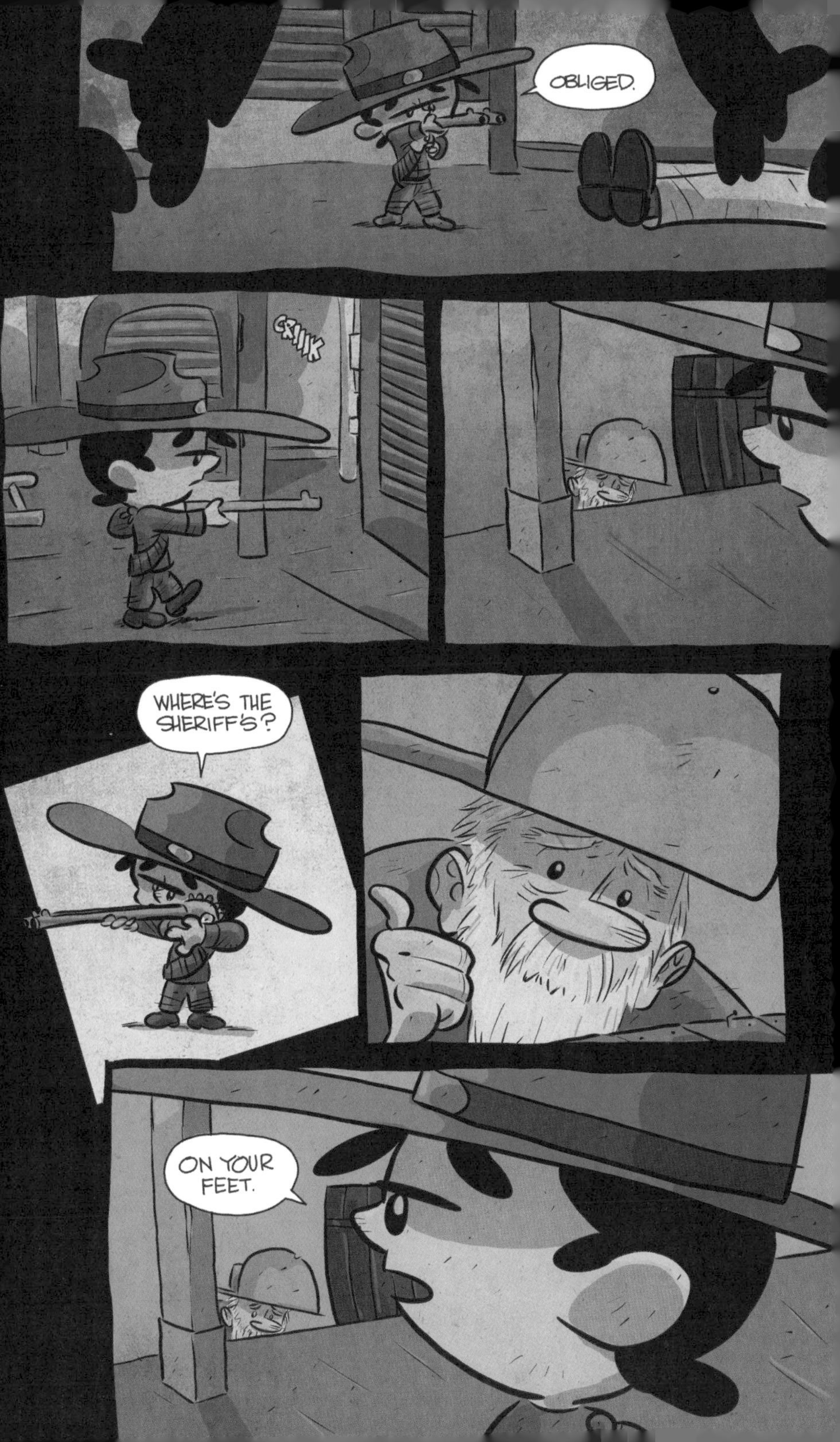
OBLIGED.
CRIIIK
WHERE'S THE SHERIFF'S?
ON YOUR FEET.

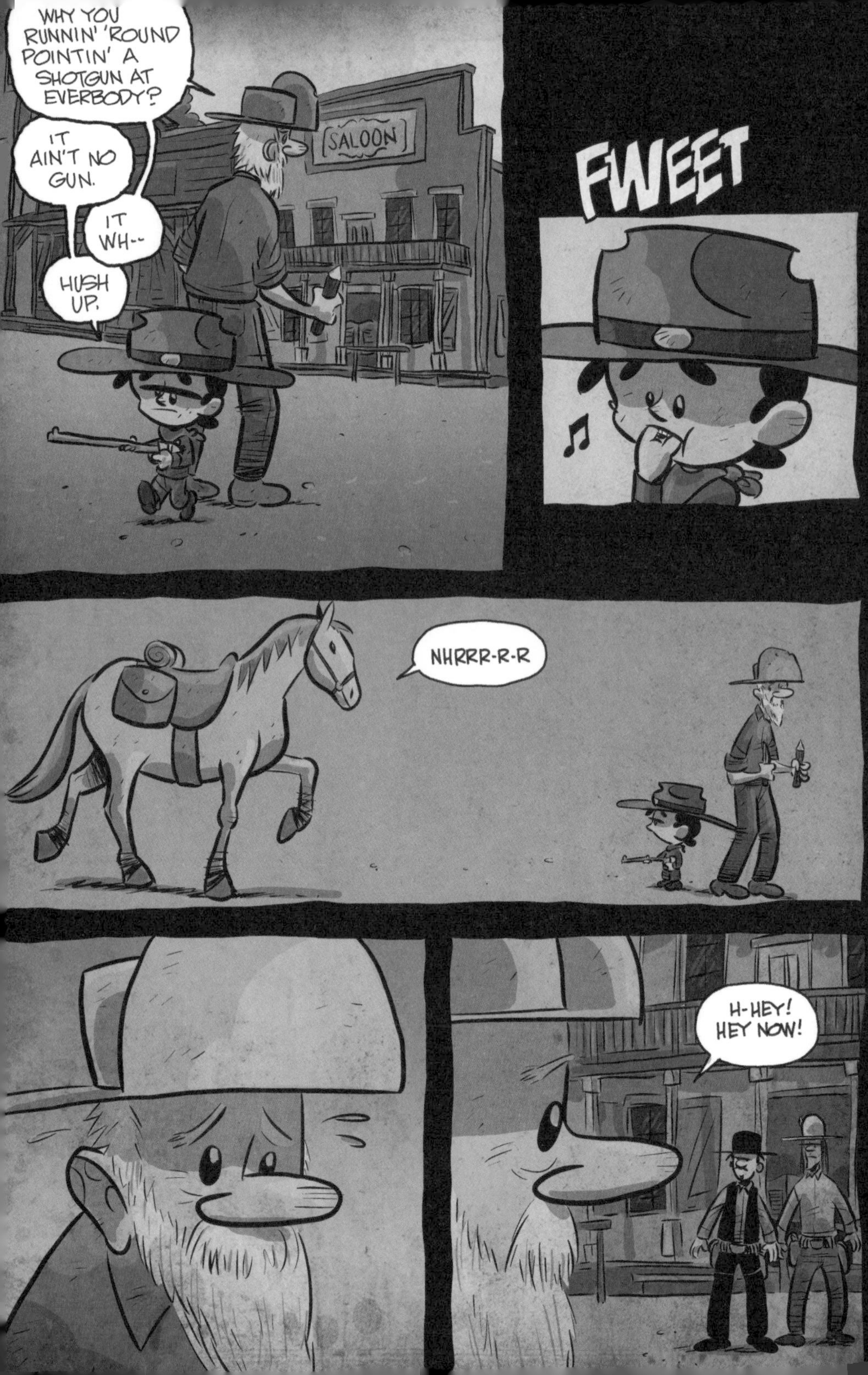
WHY YOU RUNNIN' 'ROUND POINTIN' A SHOTGUN AT EVERBODY?
IT AIN'T NO GUN.
IT WH--
HUSH UP.
SALOON
FWEET
NHRRR-R-R
H-HEY! HEY NOW!

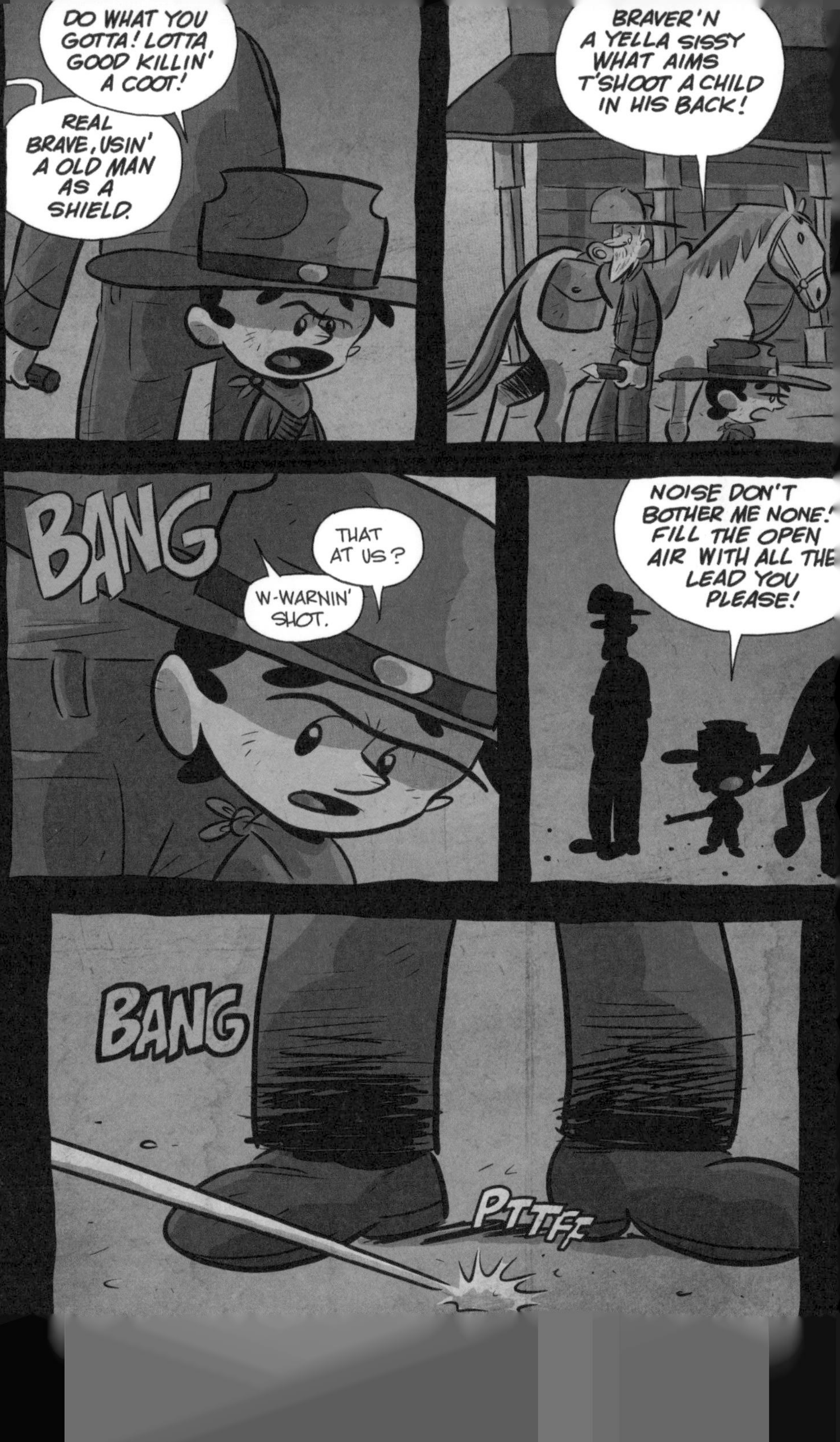

DO WHAT YOU GOTTA! LOTTA GOOD KILLIN' A COOT!
REAL BRAVE, USIN' A OLD MAN AS A SHIELD.
BRAVER'N A YELLA SISSY WHAT AIMS T'SHOOT A CHILD IN HIS BACK!
BANG
THAT AT US?
W-WARNIN' SHOT.
NOISE DON'T BOTHER ME NONE! FILL THE OPEN AIR WITH ALL THE LEAD YOU PLEASE!
BANG
PTTFF

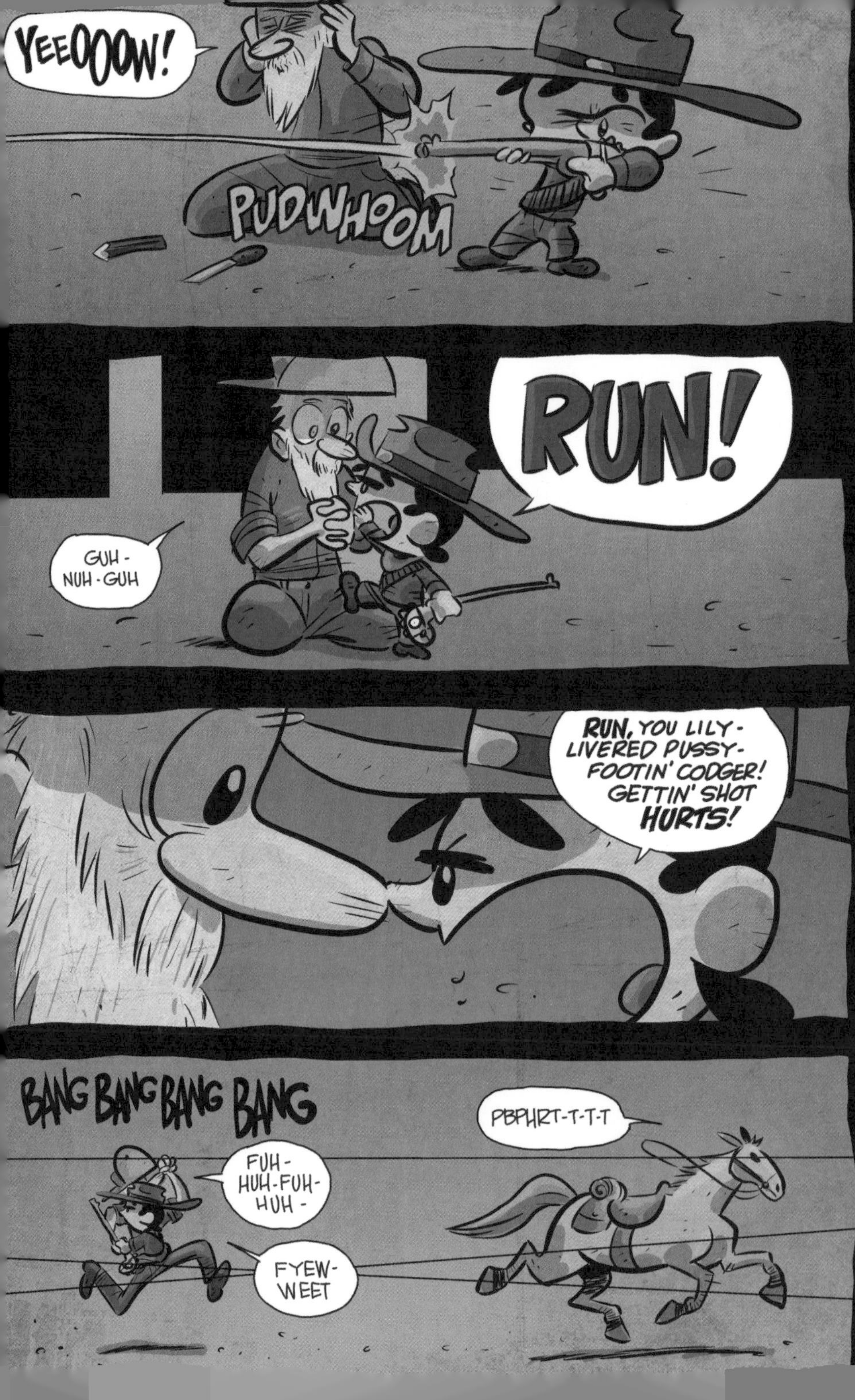
YEEOOOW!
PUDWHOOM
RUN!
GUH-NUH-GUH
RUN, YOU LILY-LIVERED PUSSY-FOOTIN' CODGER! GETTIN' SHOT HURTS!
BANG BANG BANG BANG
FUH-HUH-FUH-HUH-
FYEW-WEET
PBPHRT-T-T-T

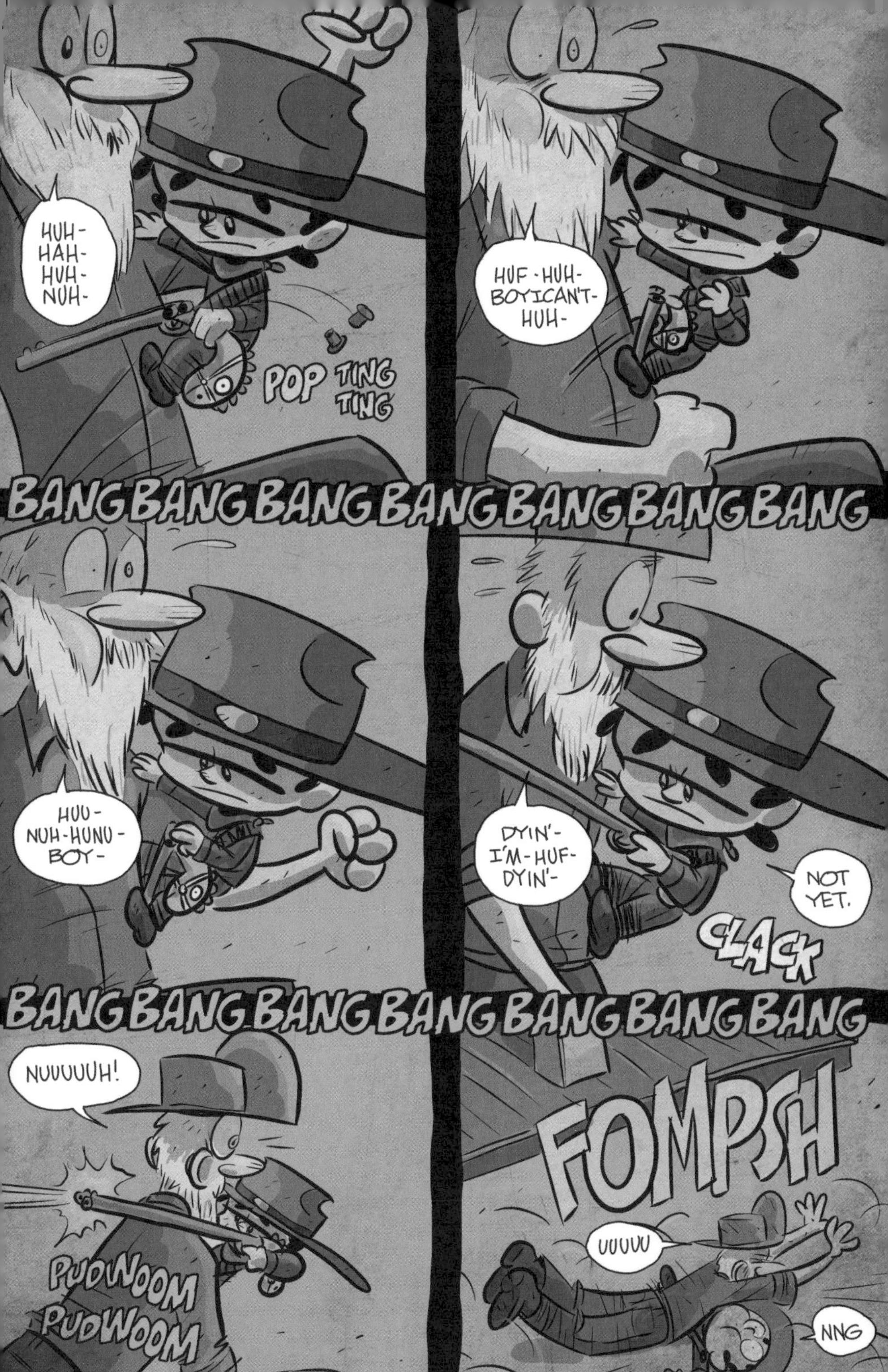
HUH-HAH-HUH-NUH-
POP TING TING
HUF-HUH-BOY I CAN'T-HUH-
BANG BANG BANG BANG BANG BANG BANG
HUU-NUH-HUNU-BOY-
DYIN'-I'M-HUF-DYIN'-
NOT YET.
CLACK
BANG BANG BANG BANG BANG BANG BANG
NUUUUUH!
PUDWOOM PUDWOOM
FOMPSH
UUUUU
NNG

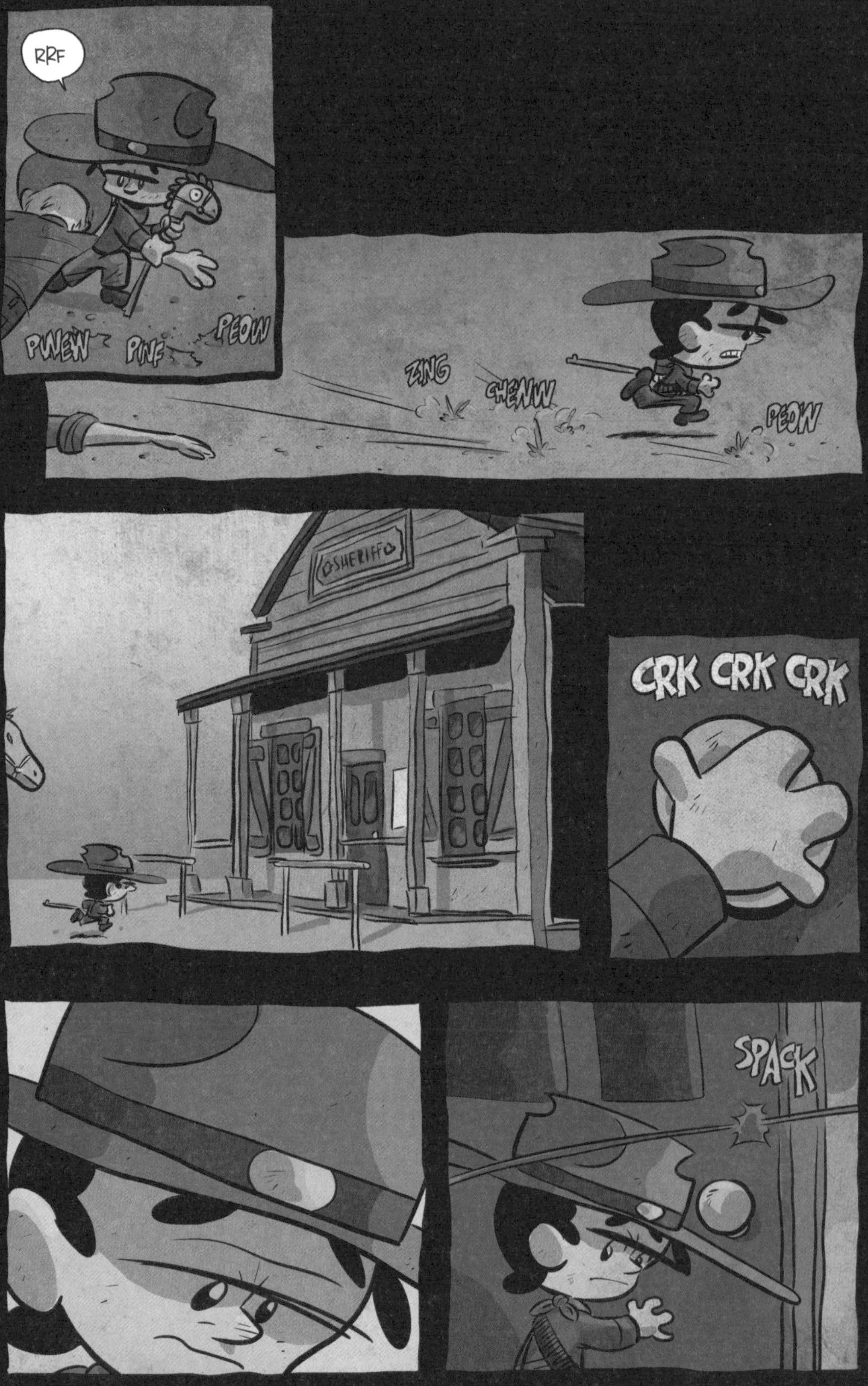
RRF
PWEW
PINF
PEOW
ZING
CHENW
PEOW
SHERIFF
CRK CRK CRK
SPACK

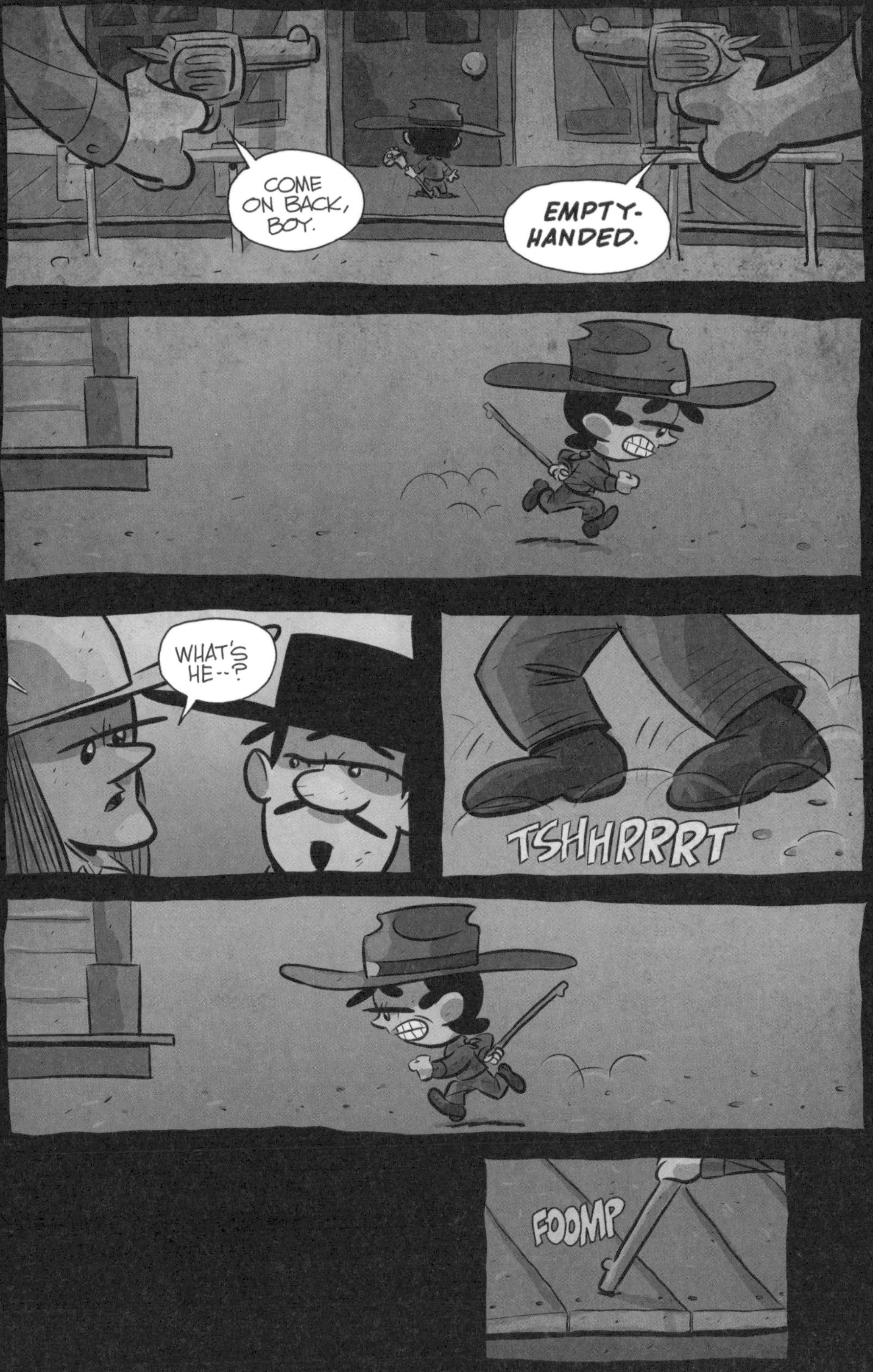
COME ON BACK, BOY.
EMPTY-HANDED.
WHAT'S HE--?
TSHHRRRT
FOOMP

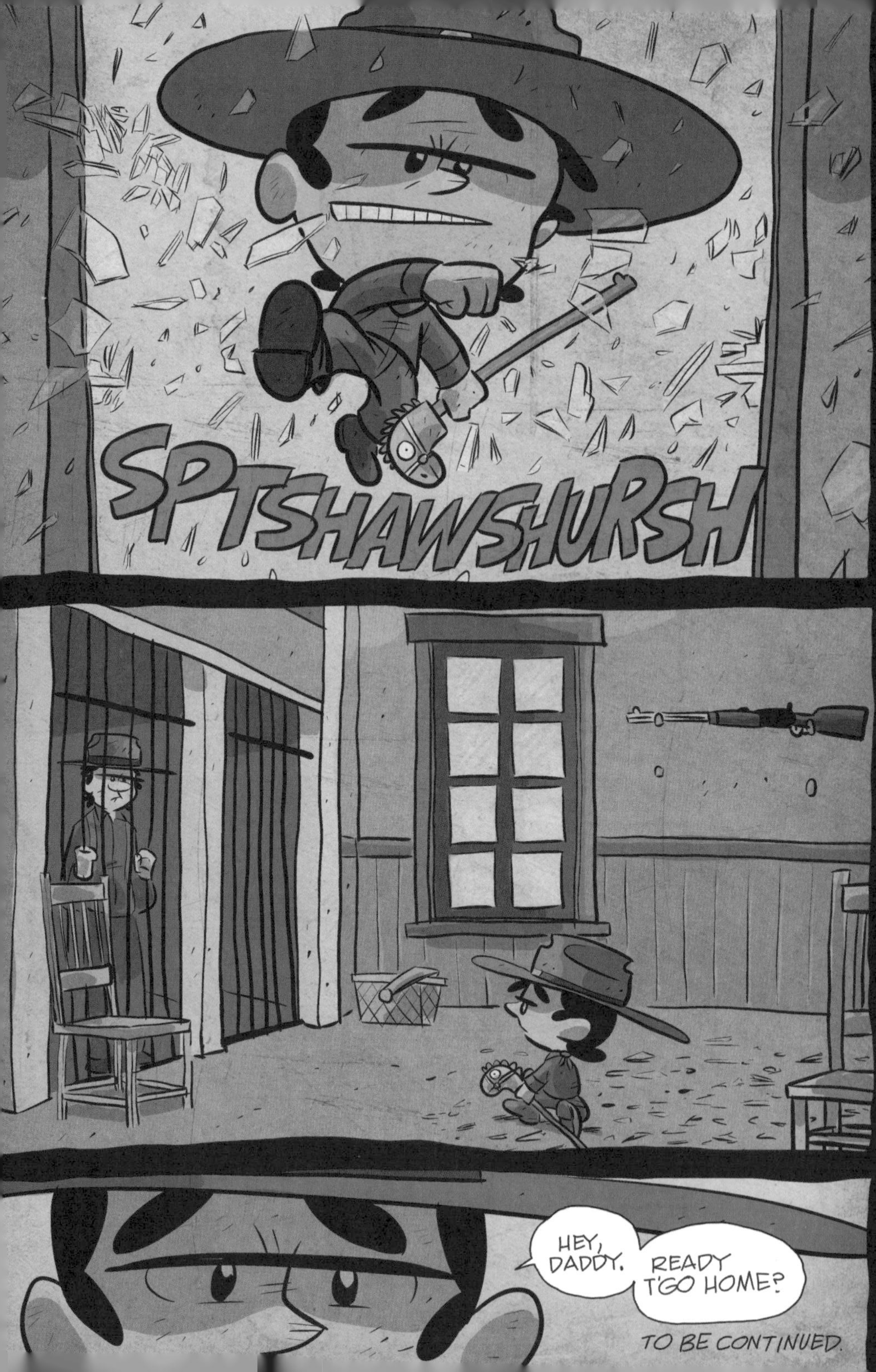
SPTSHAWSHURSH
HEY, DADDY.
READY T'GO HOME?
TO BE CONTINUED.

I'M MEAN. I'M ORNERY. WHEN I GET RILED, EVEN THE **RATTLESNAKES** SHIVER.

BUT I GOT A GOOD REASON — 'CUZ THAT LOW-DOWN DIRTY SNEAK, **BIG BILL PANTYWAIST,** DONE ME WRONG. AND EVER SINCE THEN, I'VE SUFFERED FROM THE MOST **TERRIBLE** CHAFING. Y'SEE... THEY CALL ME...

THE MAN WITH NO UNDERPANTS

THAT TUNE... HOW IT HAUNTS ME. EVER SINCE I WAS KIDNAPPED AS A BOY BY THAT **NAVAJO BRASS BAND,** NOT A MOMENT GOES BY WHEN I DON'T HEAR THE **WILLIAM TELL OVERTURE** RINGING IN MY EARS.

dagga dump ♪
dagga dump
dagga dump
♫ dump ♪
dump

BUT SOON IT WOULD ALL BE OVER. SOON I'D CATCH UP WITH BIG BILL... AND THEN MAYBE I'D PUT SOME OF THOSE **DEMONS** TO REST.

GEE-UP, PORKY!

UNPLEASANT GULCH

WAIT HERE.

HARD LUCK SALOON

squonk

P.TOO

GASP!

MAN WITH UNDE

ITH NDERPANTS

MAN W NO UNDE

MAN WITH NO UNDERPANTS

MAN NO UNDE

MAN WITH NO UNDERPANTS

MAN WITH NO UNDERPANTS

ALL RIGHT! BRING ME **BIG BILL PANTYWAIST...** OR THERE'LL... BE TROUBLE!

PLOINK

SOMEBODY BRING THAT THING CLOSER.

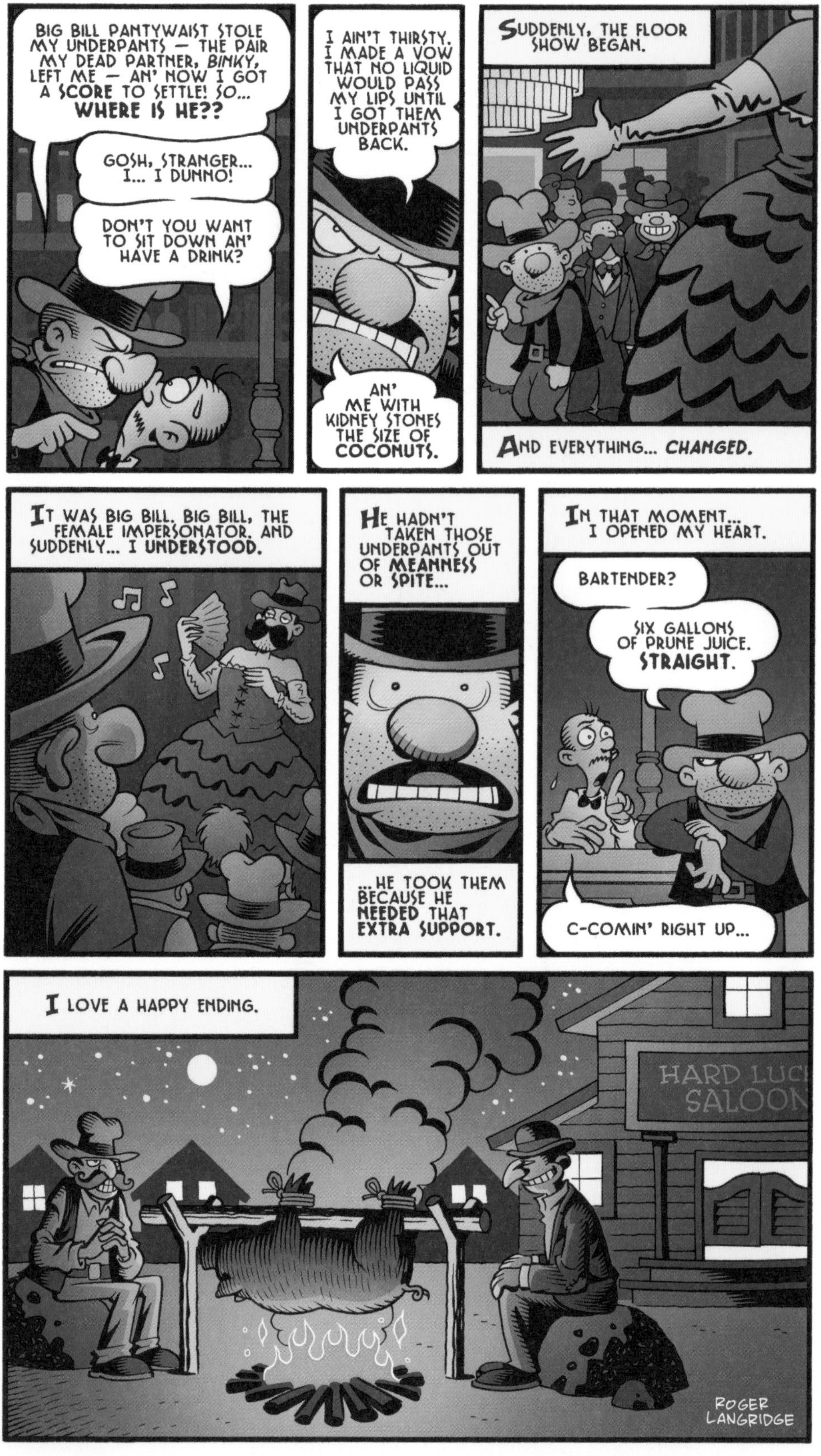
BIG BILL PANTYWAIST STOLE MY UNDERPANTS — THE PAIR MY DEAD PARTNER, *BINKY*, LEFT ME — AN' NOW I GOT A **SCORE** TO SETTLE! SO... **WHERE IS HE??**
GOSH, STRANGER... I... I DUNNO!
DON'T YOU WANT TO SIT DOWN AN' HAVE A DRINK?
I AIN'T THIRSTY. I MADE A VOW THAT NO LIQUID WOULD PASS MY LIPS UNTIL I GOT THEM UNDERPANTS BACK.
AN' ME WITH KIDNEY STONES THE SIZE OF **COCONUTS.**
SUDDENLY, THE FLOOR SHOW BEGAN.
AND EVERYTHING... ***CHANGED.***
IT WAS BIG BILL. BIG BILL, THE FEMALE IMPERSONATOR. AND SUDDENLY... I **UNDERSTOOD.**
HE HADN'T TAKEN THOSE UNDERPANTS OUT OF **MEANNESS** OR **SPITE...**
...HE TOOK THEM BECAUSE HE **NEEDED** THAT **EXTRA SUPPORT.**
IN THAT MOMENT... I OPENED MY HEART.
BARTENDER?
SIX GALLONS OF PRUNE JUICE. **STRAIGHT.**
C-COMIN' RIGHT UP...
I LOVE A HAPPY ENDING.
HARD LUCK SALOON
ROGER LANGRIDGE

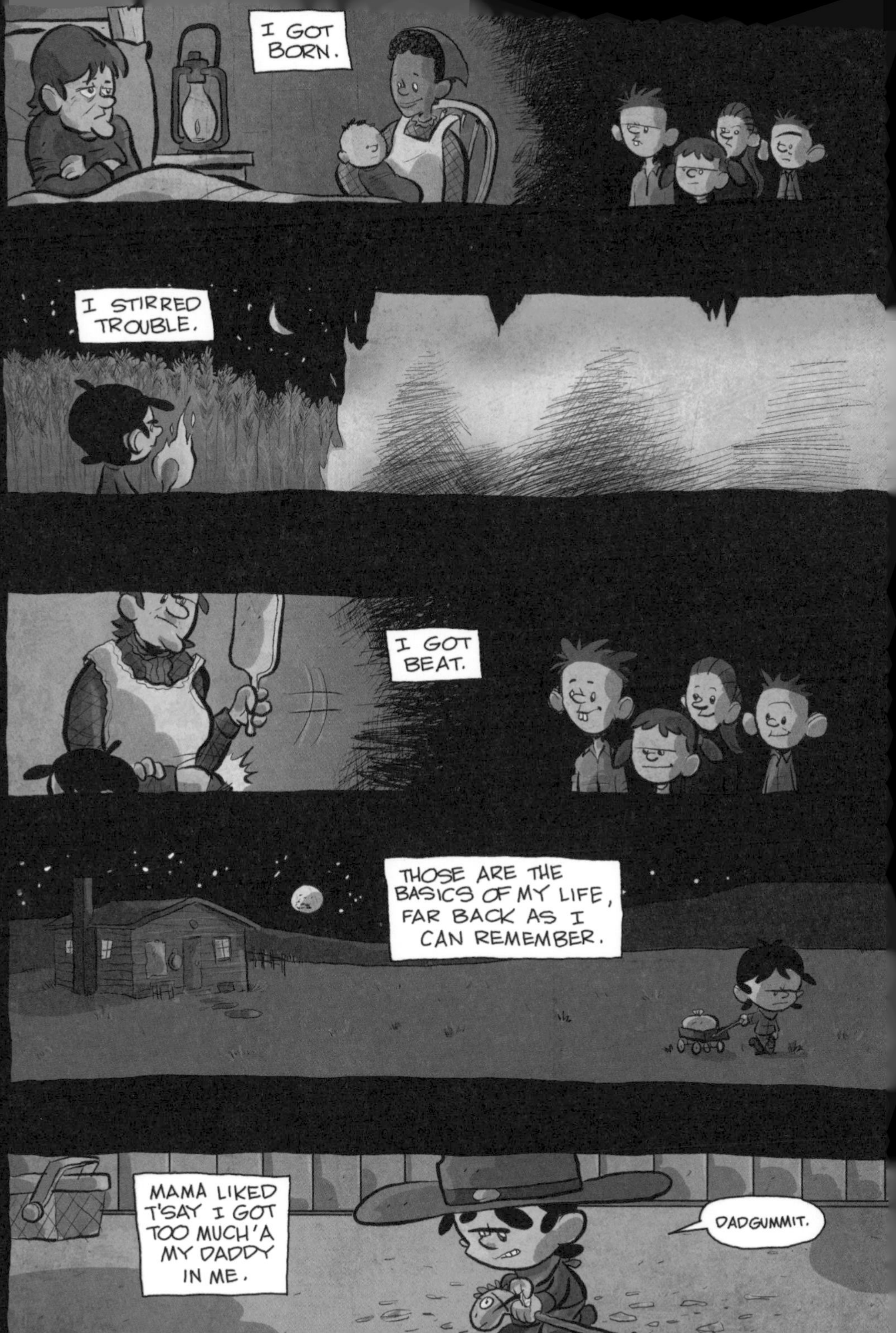
I GOT BORN.
I STIRRED TROUBLE.
I GOT BEAT.
THOSE ARE THE BASICS OF MY LIFE, FAR BACK AS I CAN REMEMBER.
MAMA LIKED T'SAY I GOT TOO MUCH'A MY DADDY IN ME.
DADGUMMIT.

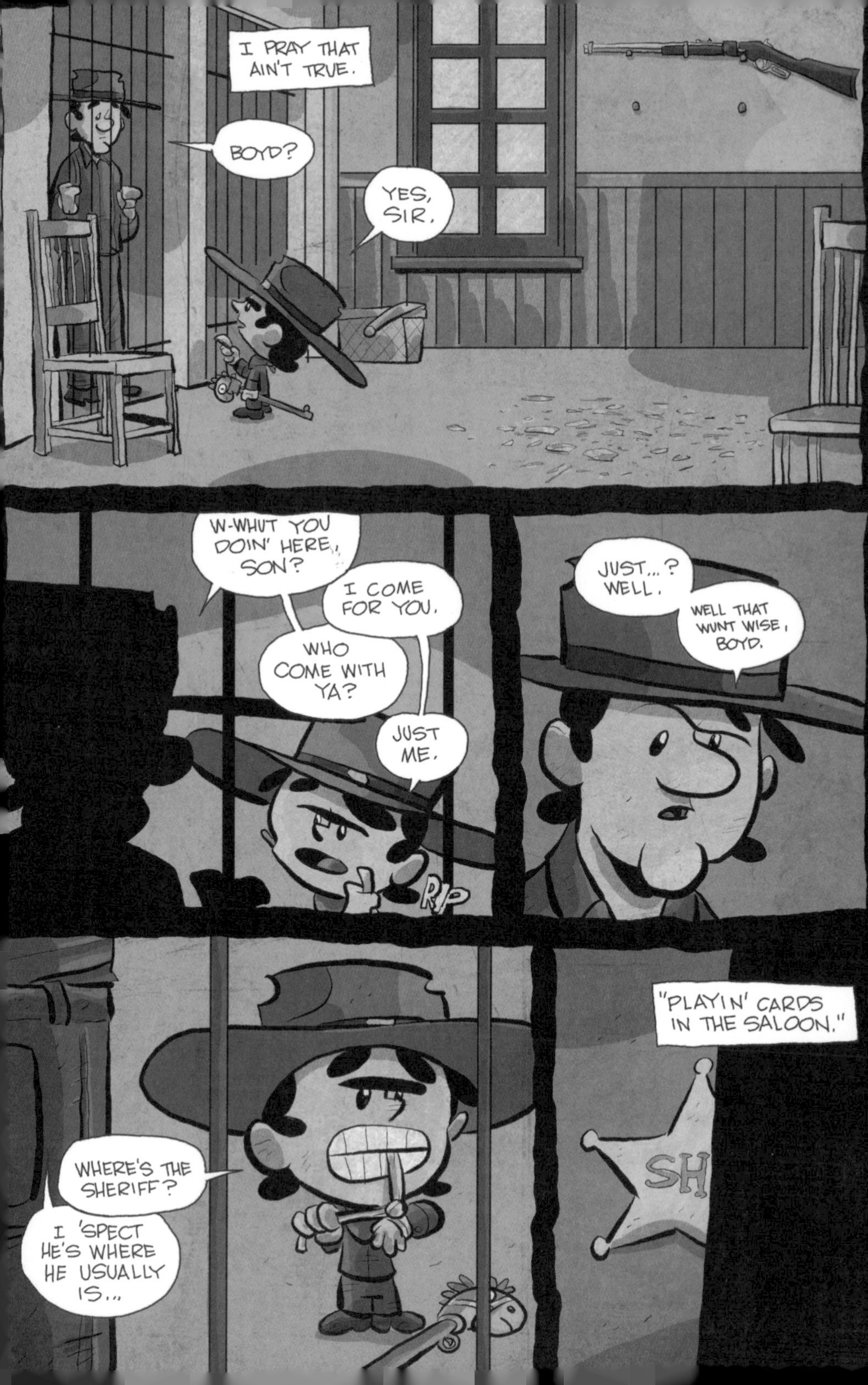

I PRAY THAT AIN'T TRUE.
BOYD?
YES, SIR.
W-WHUT YOU DOIN' HERE, SON?
I COME FOR YOU.
WHO COME WITH YA?
JUST ME.
RIP
JUST...? WELL.
WELL THAT WUNT WISE, BOYD.
WHERE'S THE SHERIFF?
I 'SPECT HE'S WHERE HE USUALLY IS...
"PLAYIN' CARDS IN THE SALOON."
SH

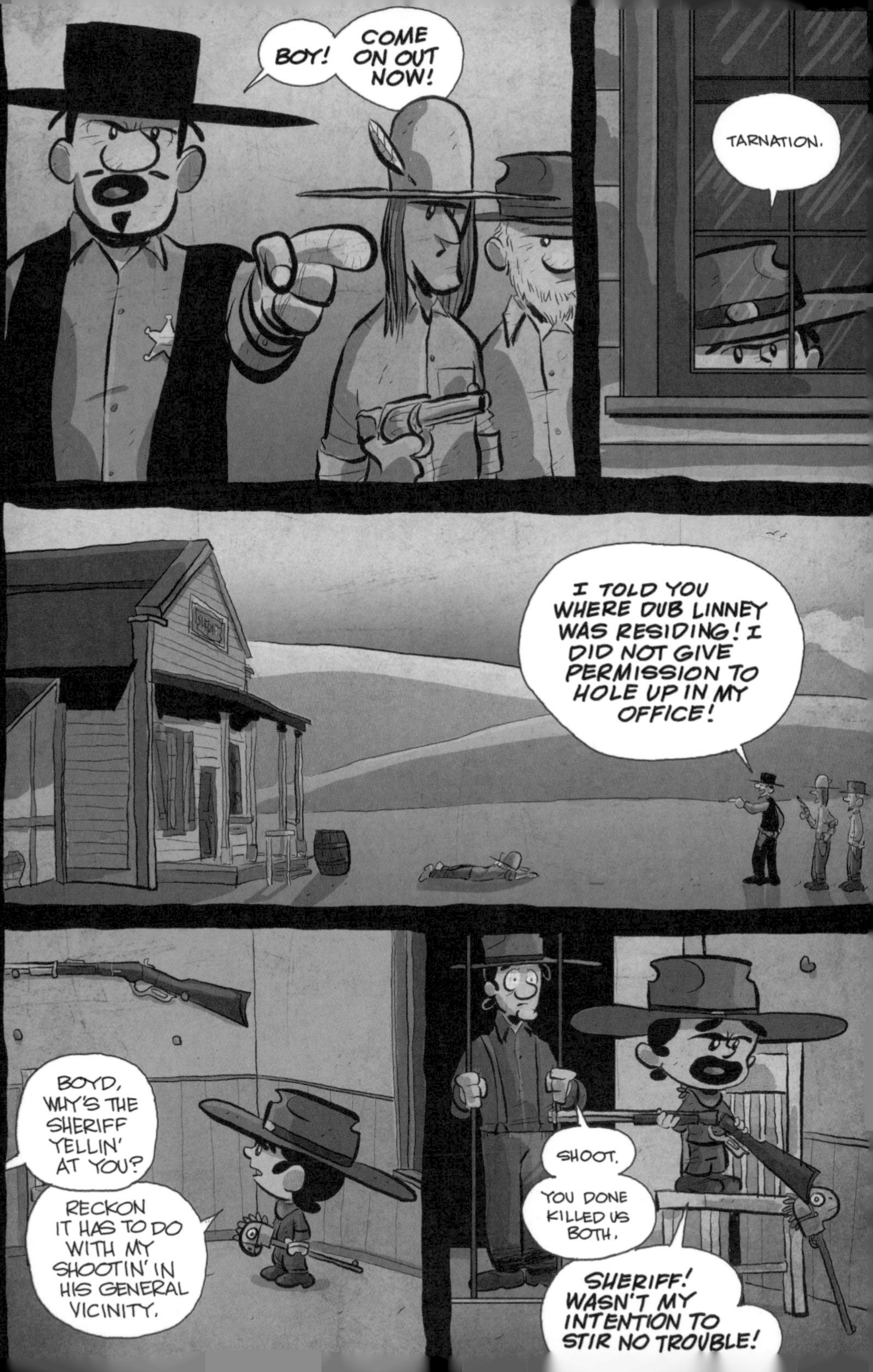
BOY!
COME ON OUT NOW!
TARNATION.
I TOLD YOU WHERE DUB LINNEY WAS RESIDING! I DID NOT GIVE PERMISSION TO HOLE UP IN MY OFFICE!
BOYD, WHY'S THE SHERIFF YELLIN' AT YOU?
RECKON IT HAS TO DO WITH MY SHOOTIN' IN HIS GENERAL VICINITY.
SHOOT.
YOU DONE KILLED US BOTH.
SHERIFF! WASN'T MY INTENTION TO STIR NO TROUBLE!

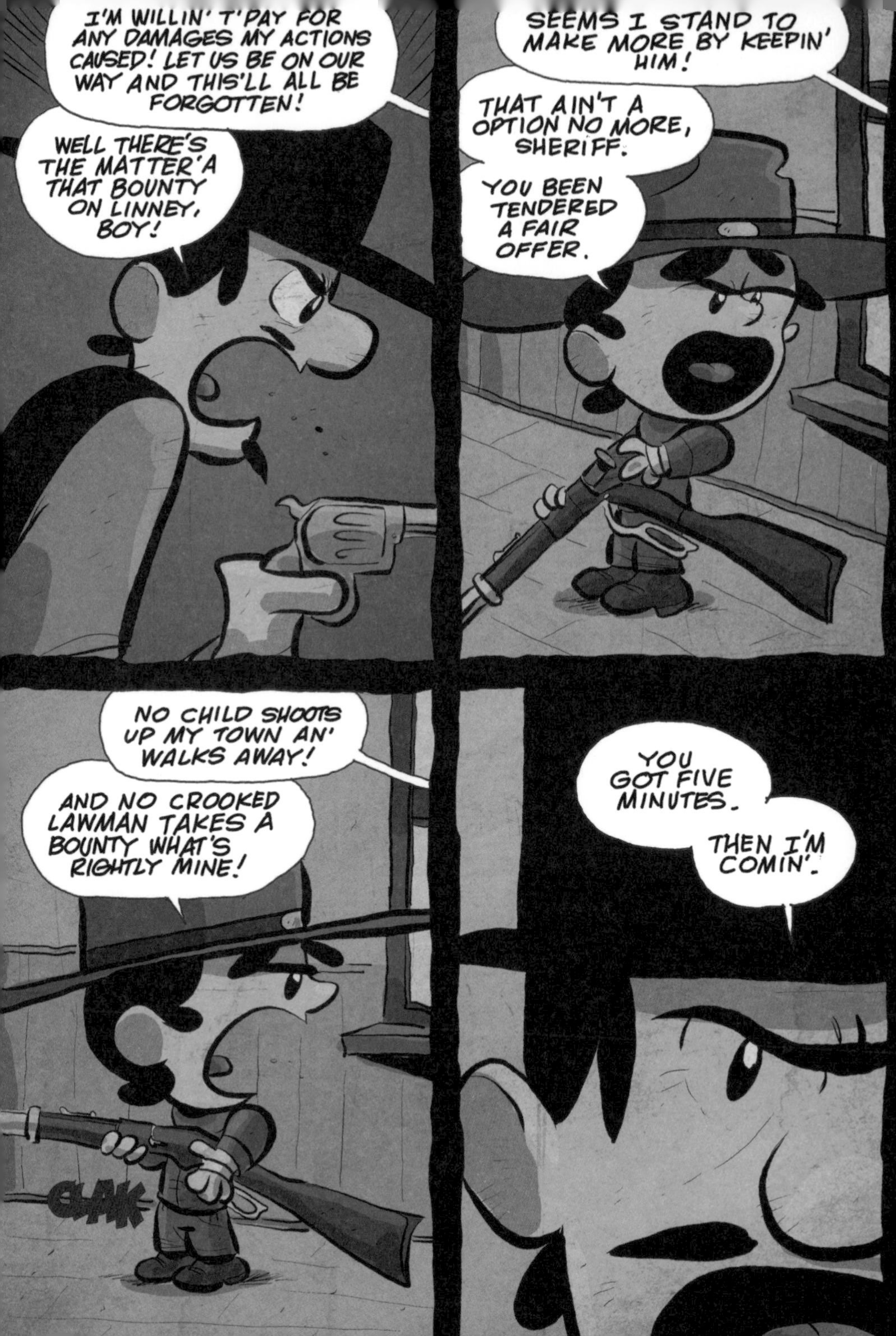
I'M WILLIN' T'PAY FOR ANY DAMAGES MY ACTIONS CAUSED! LET US BE ON OUR WAY AND THIS'LL ALL BE FORGOTTEN!
WELL THERE'S THE MATTER'A THAT BOUNTY ON LINNEY, BOY!
SEEMS I STAND TO MAKE MORE BY KEEPIN' HIM!
THAT AIN'T A OPTION NO MORE, SHERIFF.
YOU BEEN TENDERED A FAIR OFFER.
NO CHILD SHOOTS UP MY TOWN AN' WALKS AWAY!
AND NO CROOKED LAWMAN TAKES A BOUNTY WHAT'S RIGHTLY MINE!
CLAK
YOU GOT FIVE MINUTES.
THEN I'M COMIN'.

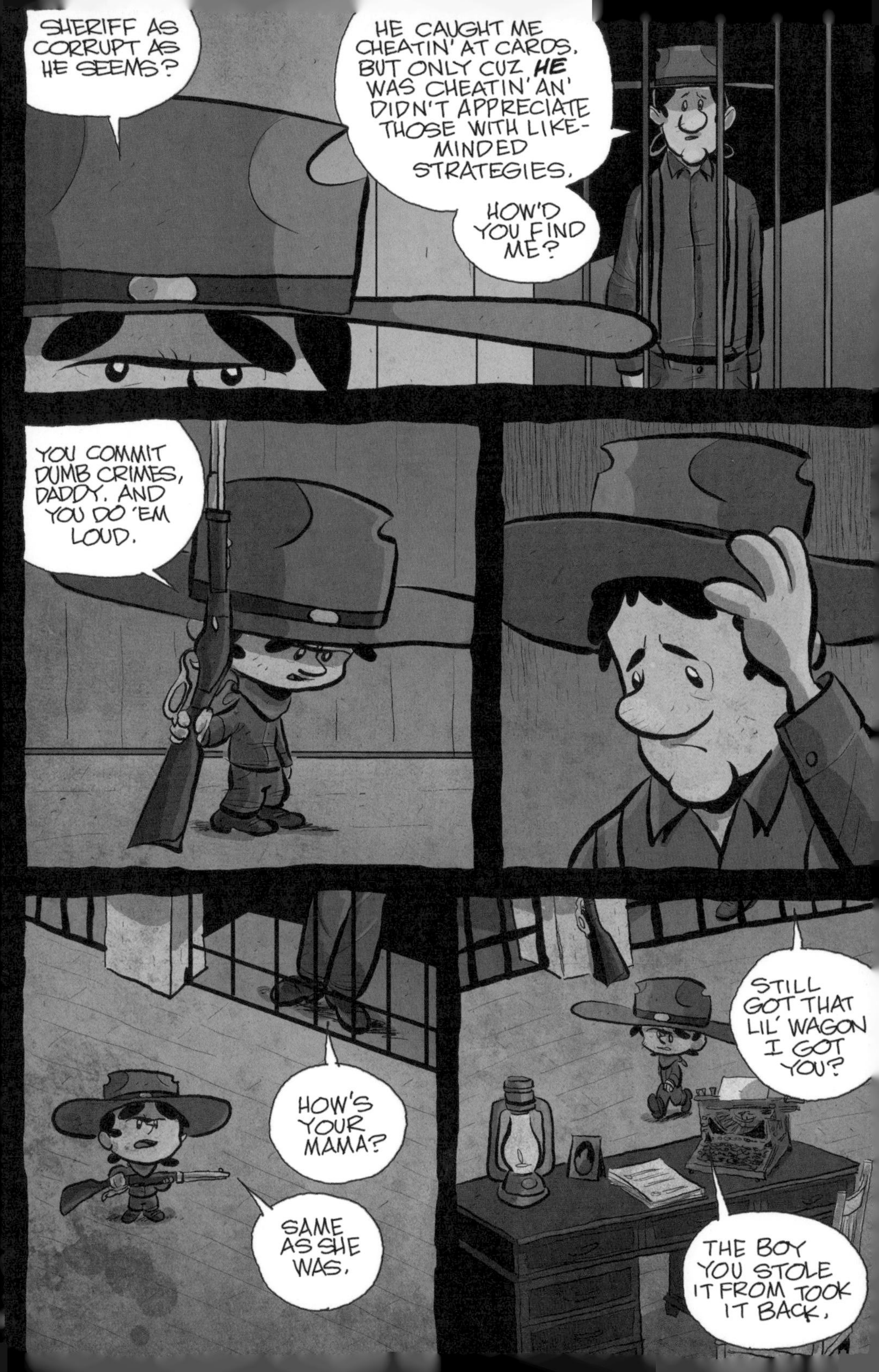
SHERIFF AS CORRUPT AS HE SEEMS?
HE CAUGHT ME CHEATIN' AT CARDS. BUT ONLY CUZ *HE* WAS CHEATIN' AN' DIDN'T APPRECIATE THOSE WITH LIKE-MINDED STRATEGIES.
HOW'D YOU FIND ME?
YOU COMMIT DUMB CRIMES, DADDY. AND YOU DO 'EM LOUD.
HOW'S YOUR MAMA?
SAME AS SHE WAS.
STILL GOT THAT LIL' WAGON I GOT YOU?
THE BOY YOU STOLE IT FROM TOOK IT BACK.

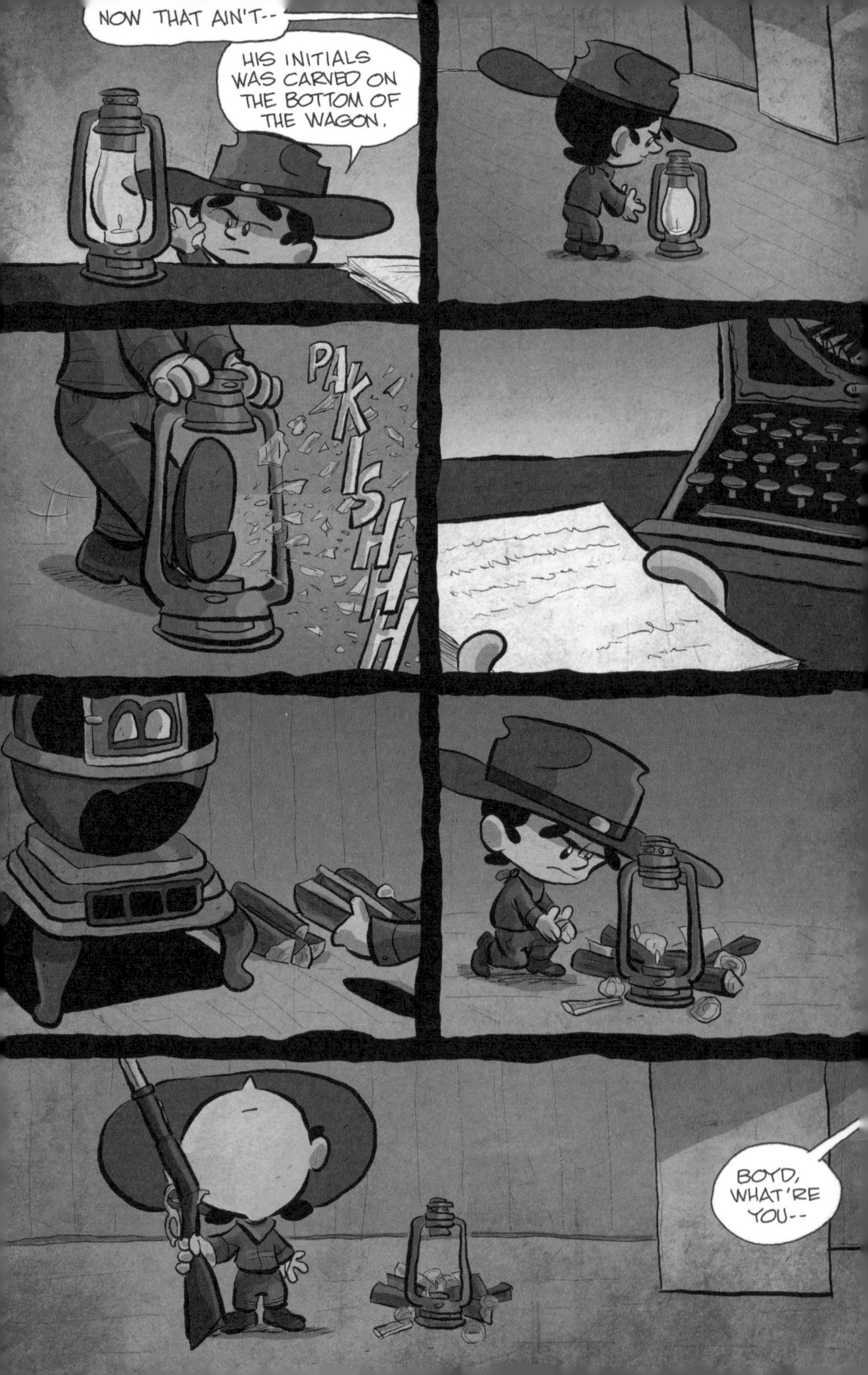
NOW THAT AIN'T--
HIS INITIALS WAS CARVED ON THE BOTTOM OF THE WAGON.
PAKISHHHH
BOYD, WHAT'RE YOU--

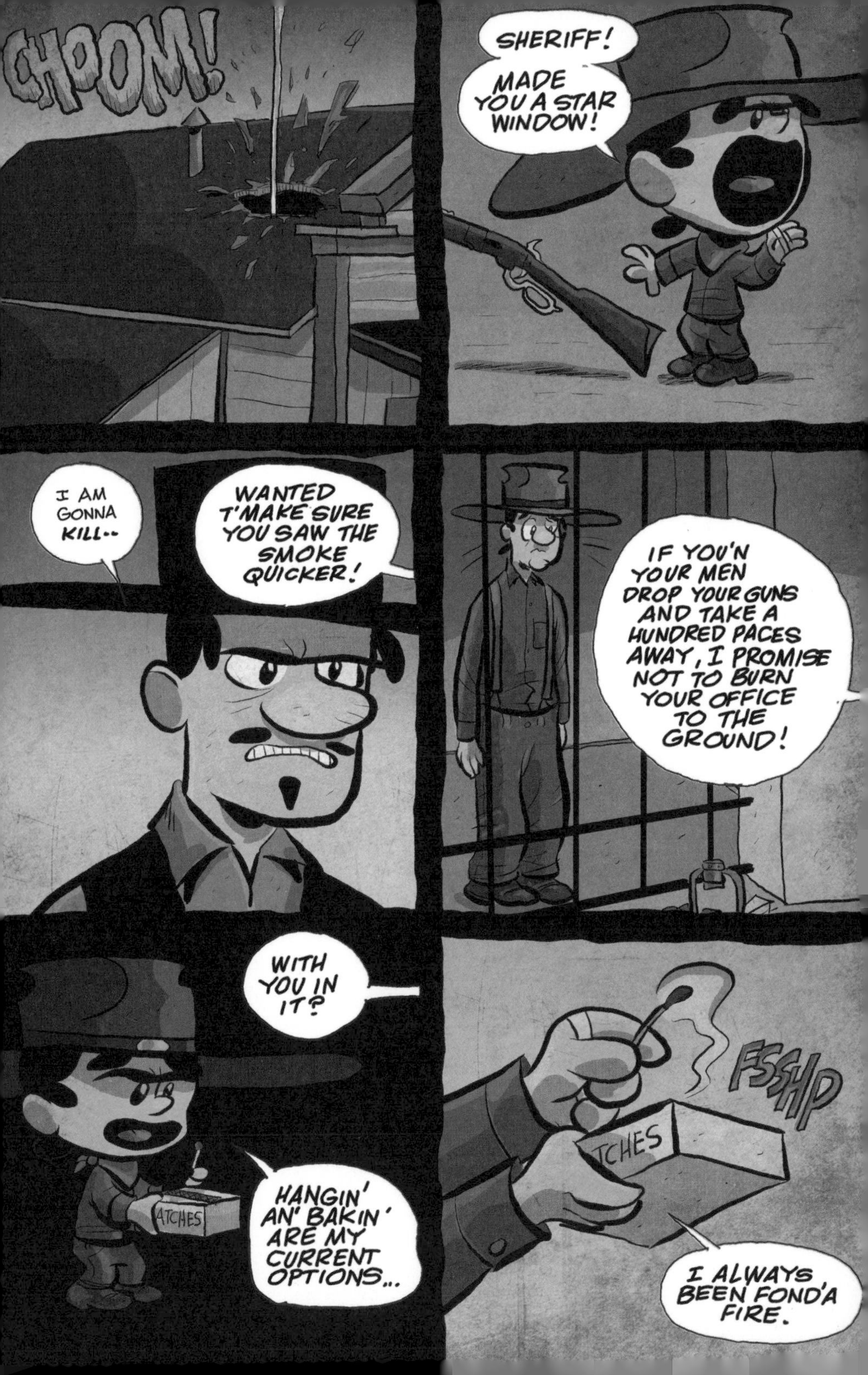

CHOOM!
SHERIFF!
MADE YOU A STAR WINDOW!
I AM GONNA KILL..
WANTED T'MAKE SURE YOU SAW THE SMOKE QUICKER!
IF YOU'N YOUR MEN DROP YOUR GUNS AND TAKE A HUNDRED PACES AWAY, I PROMISE NOT TO BURN YOUR OFFICE TO THE GROUND!
WITH YOU IN IT?
HANGIN' AN' BAKIN' ARE MY CURRENT OPTIONS...
ATCHES
FSSHP
TCHES
I ALWAYS BEEN FOND'A FIRE.

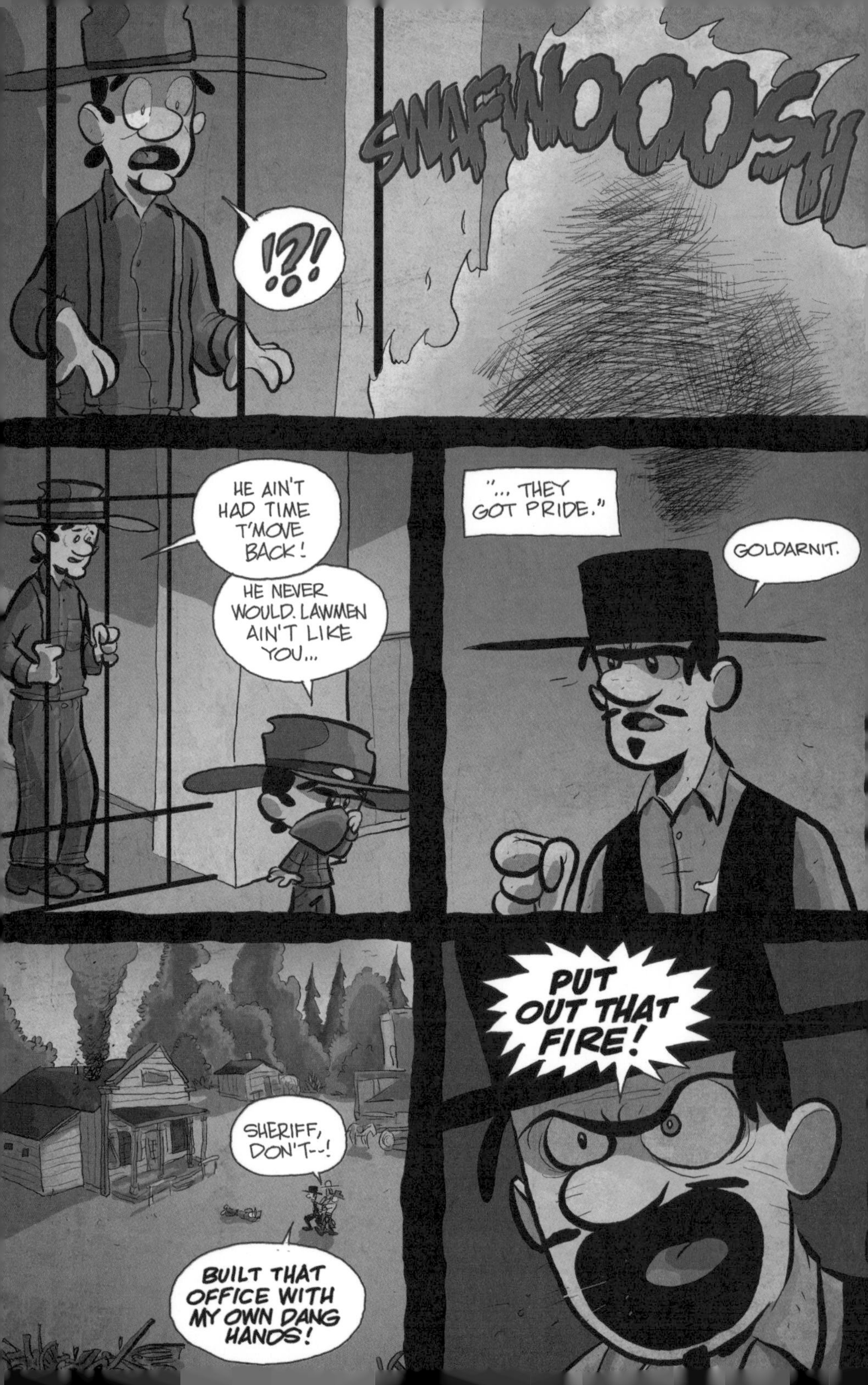
SWAFWOOOOSH
!?!
HE AIN'T HAD TIME T'MOVE BACK!
HE NEVER WOULD. LAWMEN AIN'T LIKE YOU...
"... THEY GOT PRIDE."
GOLDARNIT.
SHERIFF, DON'T--!
BUILT THAT OFFICE WITH MY OWN DANG HANDS!
PUT OUT THAT FIRE!

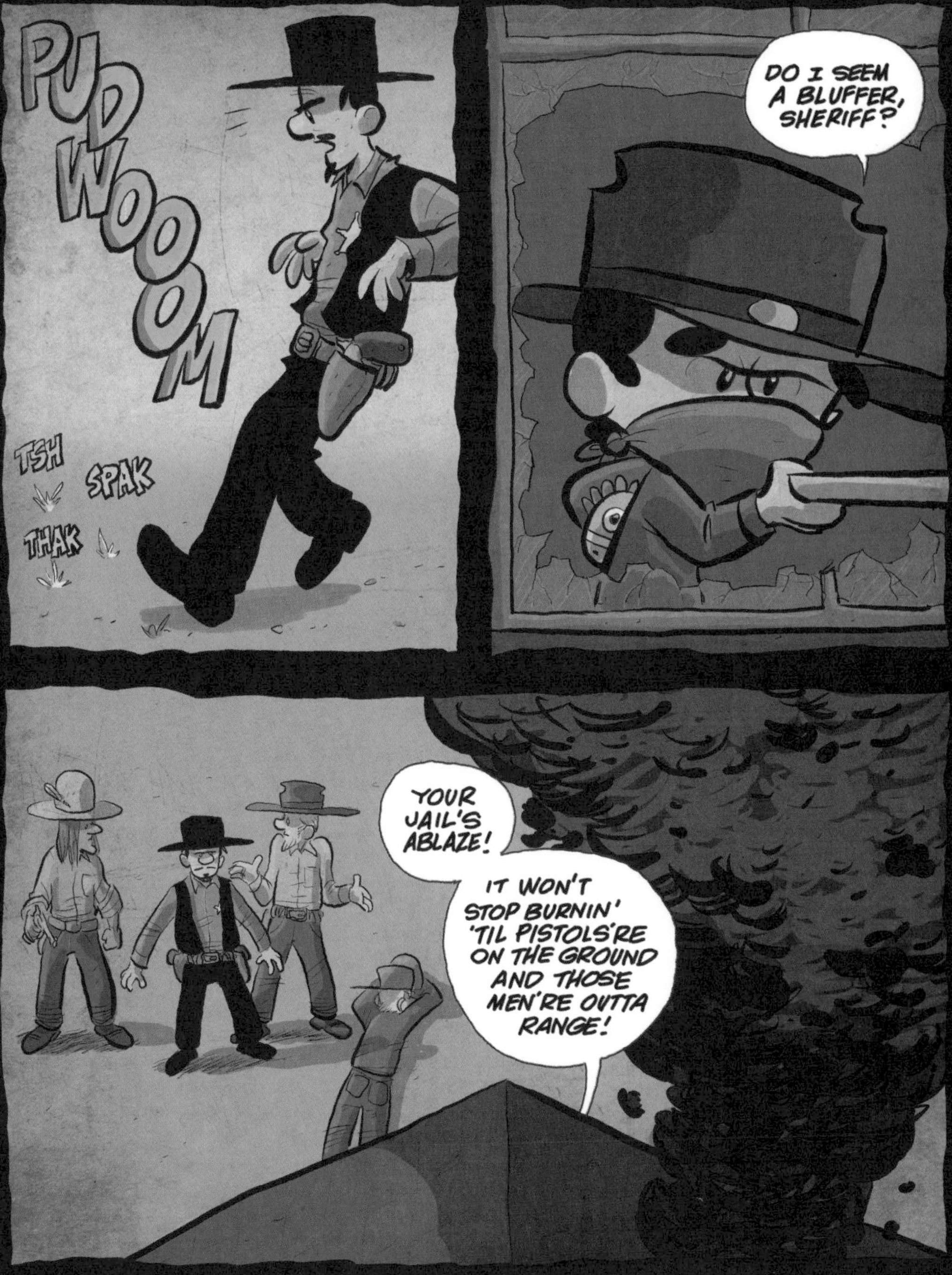
PUDWOOOOM
TSH
SPAK
THAK
DO I SEEM A BLUFFER, SHERIFF?
YOUR JAIL'S ABLAZE!
IT WON'T STOP BURNIN' 'TIL PISTOLS'RE ON THE GROUND AND THOSE MEN'RE OUTTA RANGE!

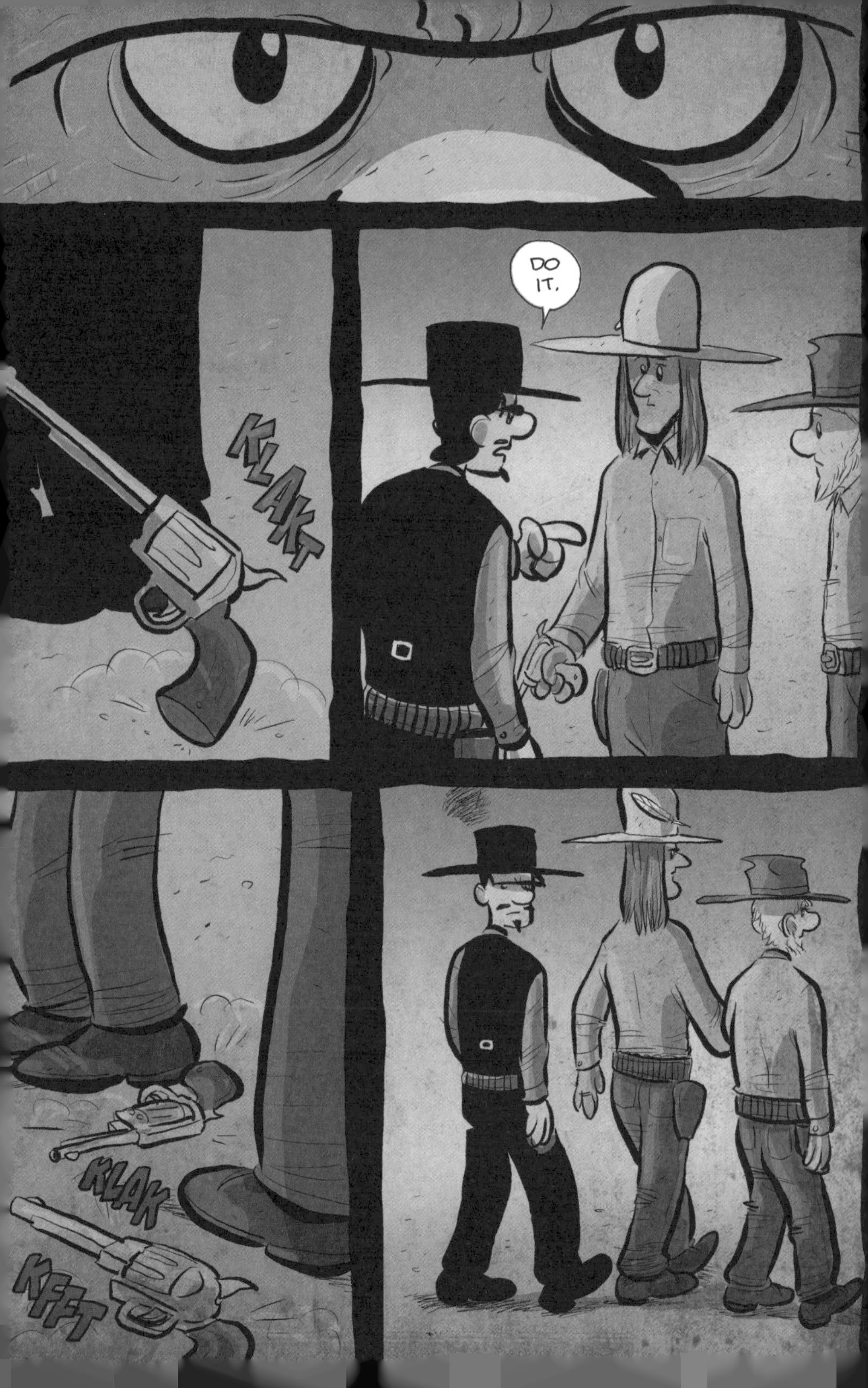
KLAKT
DO IT.
KLAK
KFFT

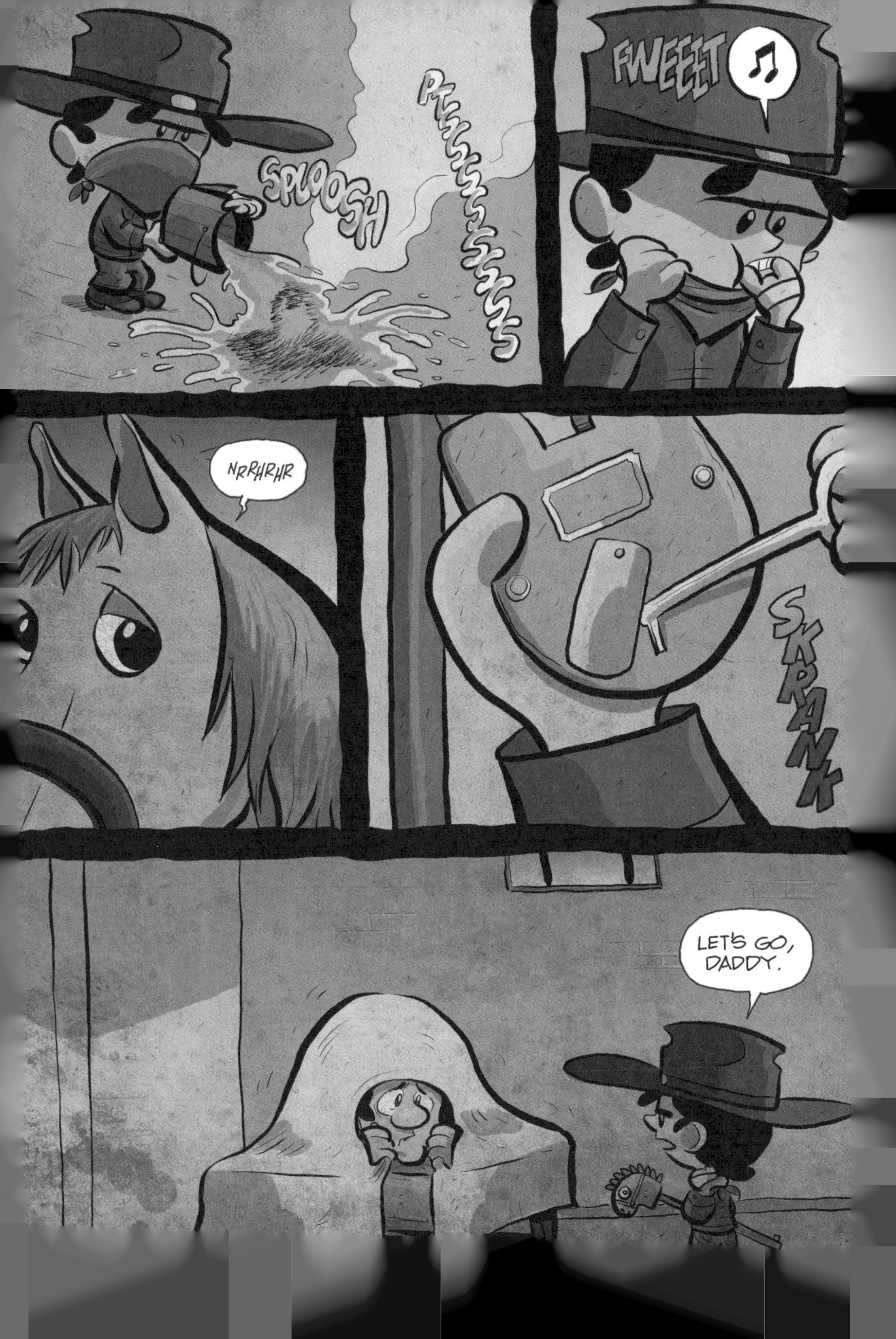
SPLOOSH
PTSSSSSSSSS
FWEEET
♫
NRRHRHR
SKRANK
LET'S GO, DADDY.

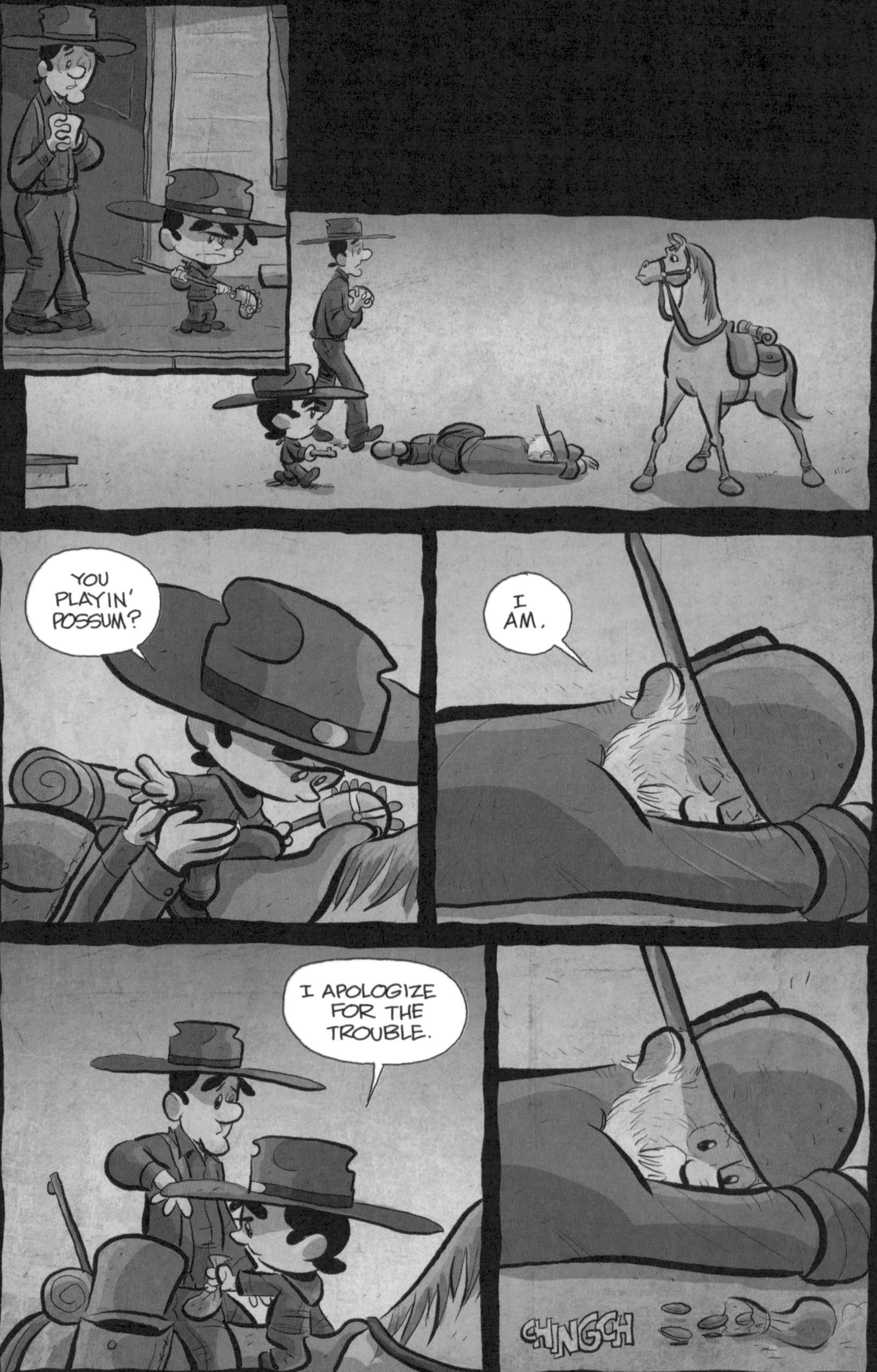
YOU PLAYIN' POSSUM?
I AM.
I APOLOGIZE FOR THE TROUBLE.
CHINGCH

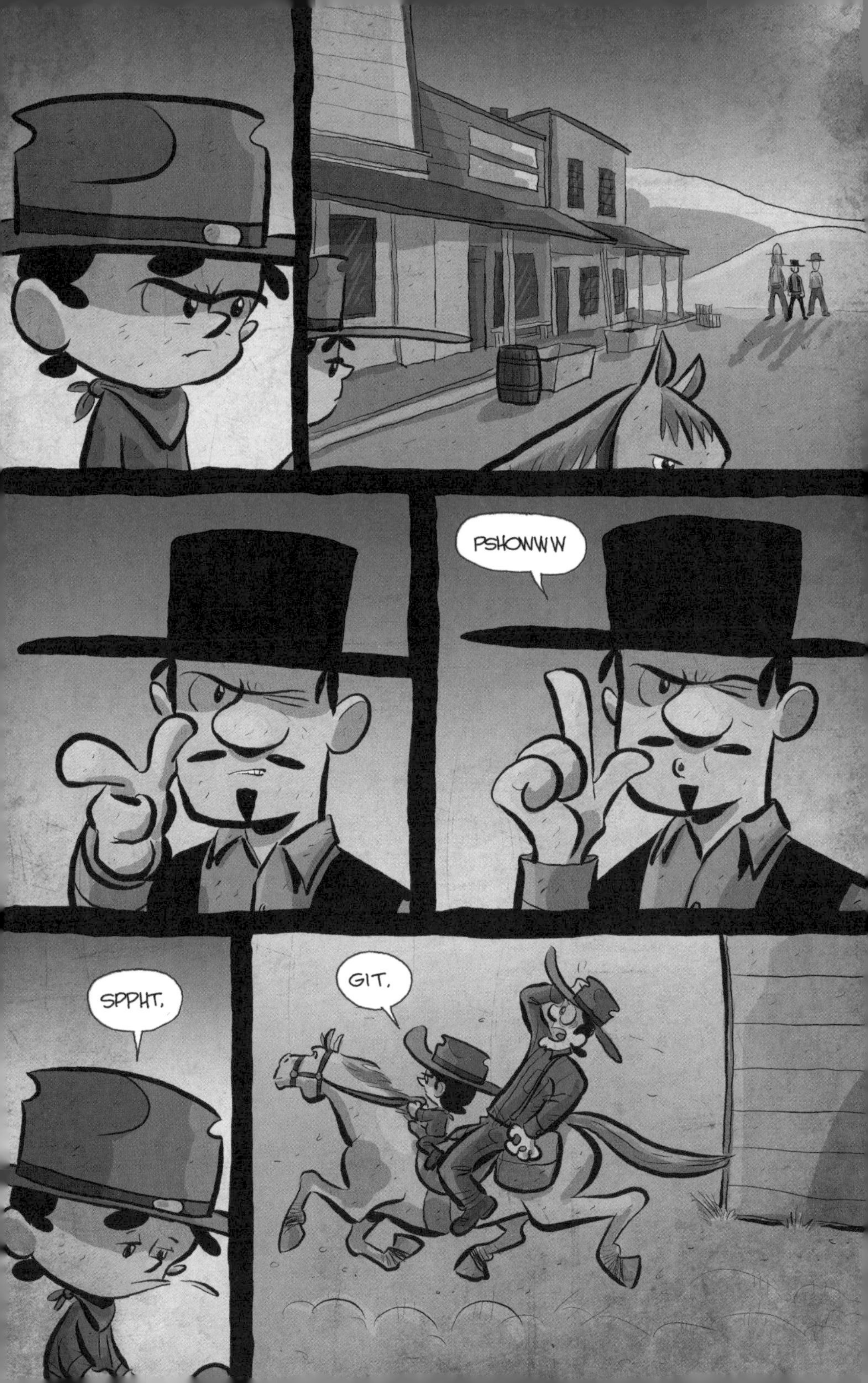
PSHOWWW
SPPHT.
GIT.

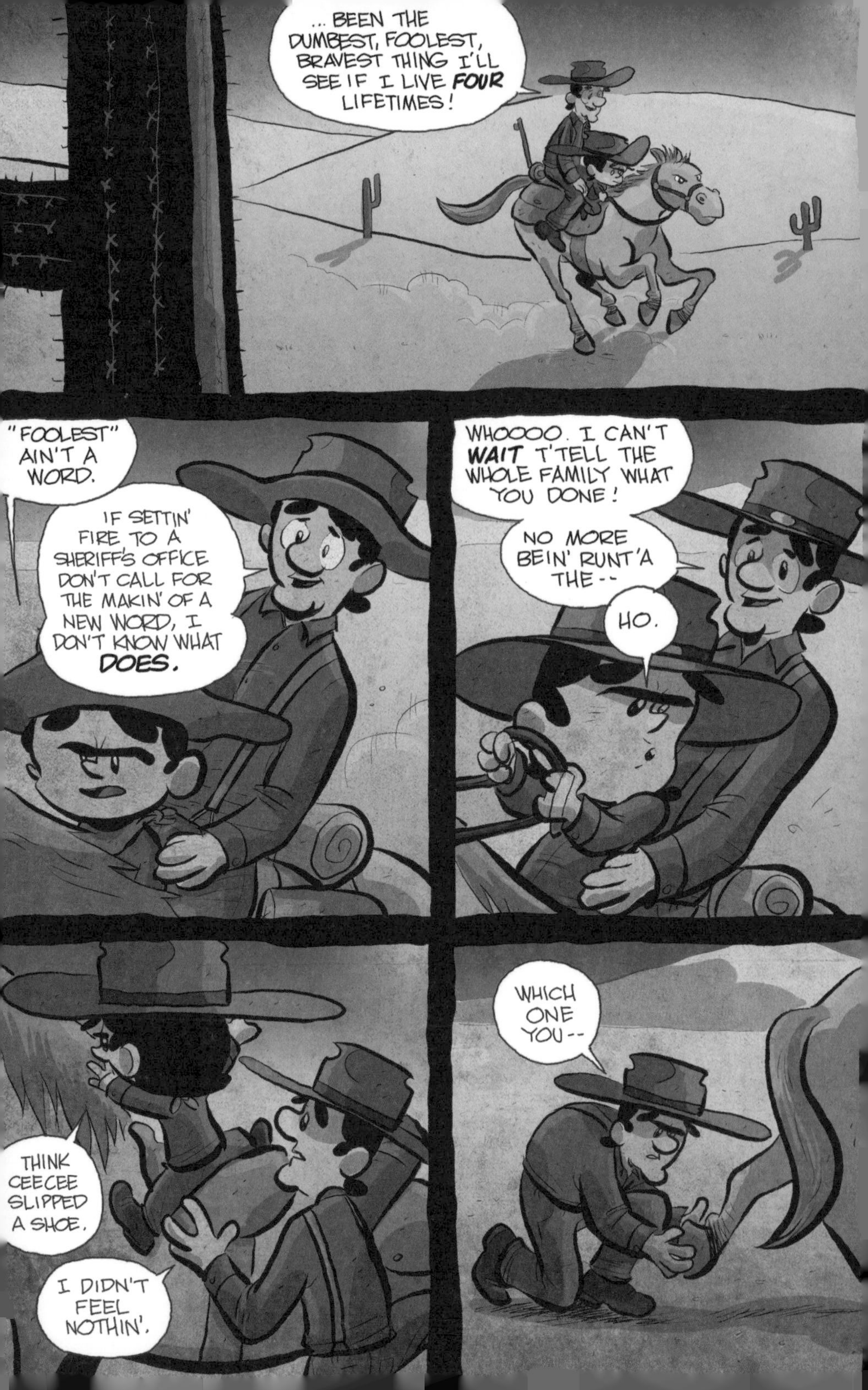
... BEEN THE DUMBEST, FOOLEST, BRAVEST THING I'LL SEE IF I LIVE FOUR LIFETIMES!
"FOOLEST" AIN'T A WORD.
IF SETTIN' FIRE TO A SHERIFF'S OFFICE DON'T CALL FOR THE MAKIN' OF A NEW WORD, I DON'T KNOW WHAT DOES.
WHOOOO. I CAN'T WAIT T'TELL THE WHOLE FAMILY WHAT YOU DONE!
NO MORE BEIN' RUNT'A THE--
HO.
THINK CEECEE SLIPPED A SHOE.
I DIDN'T FEEL NOTHIN'.
WHICH ONE YOU--

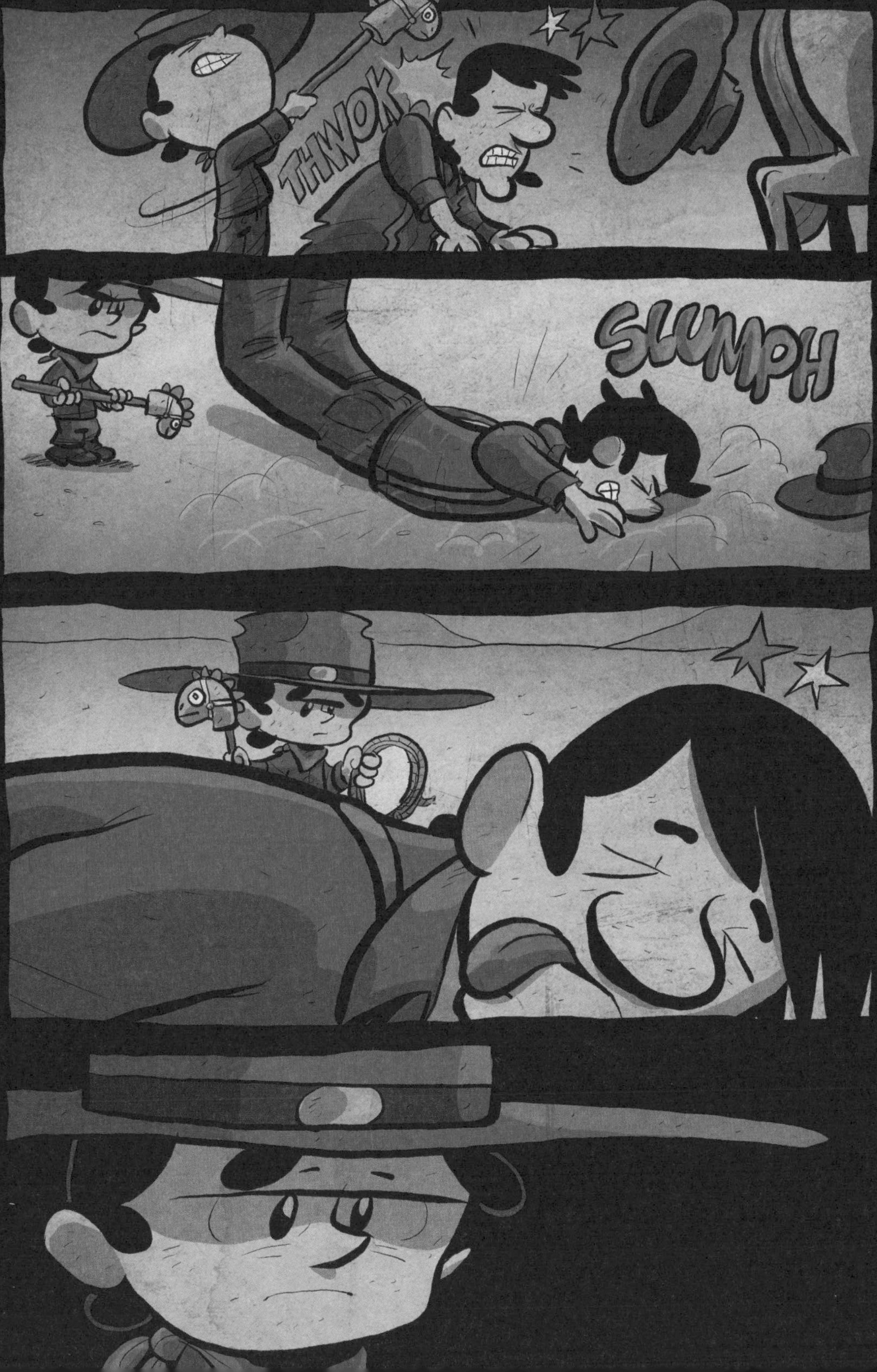
THWOK
SLUMPH

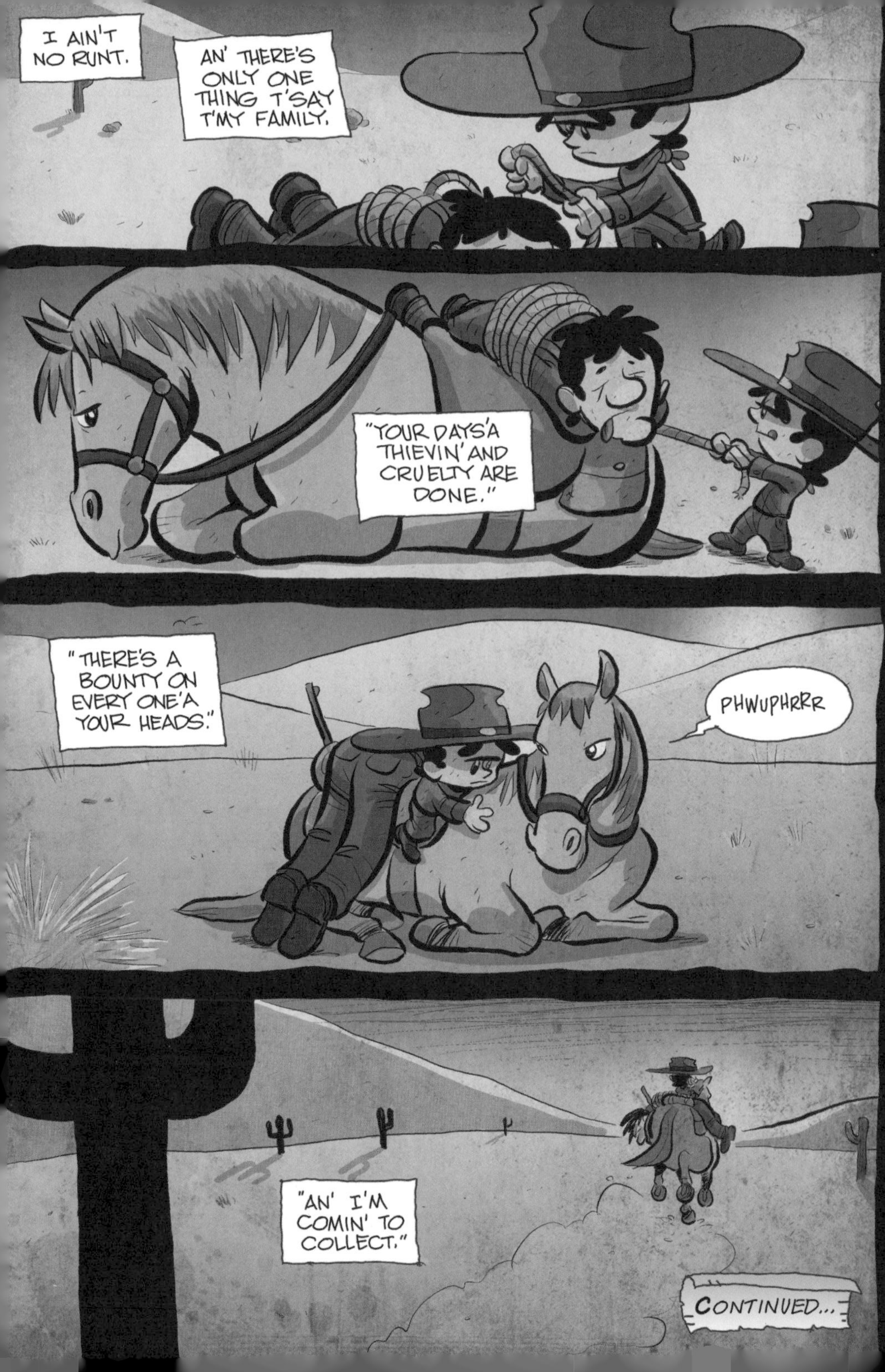
I AIN'T NO RUNT.
AN' THERE'S ONLY ONE THING T'SAY T'MY FAMILY.
"YOUR DAYS'A THIEVIN' AND CRUELTY ARE DONE."
"THERE'S A BOUNTY ON EVERY ONE'A YOUR HEADS."
PHWUPHRRR
"AN' I'M COMIN' TO COLLECT."
CONTINUED...

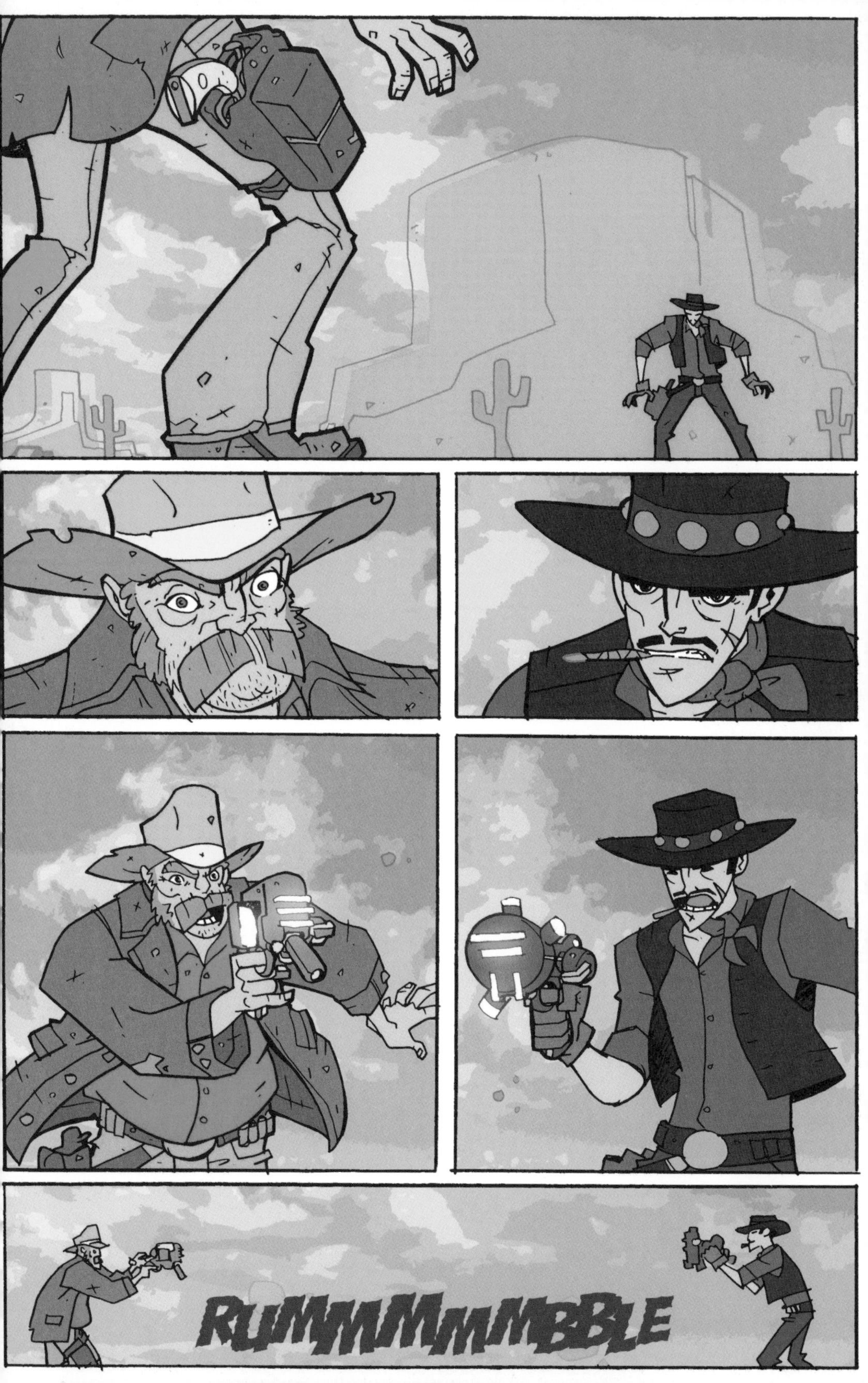
RUMMMMMMBBLE

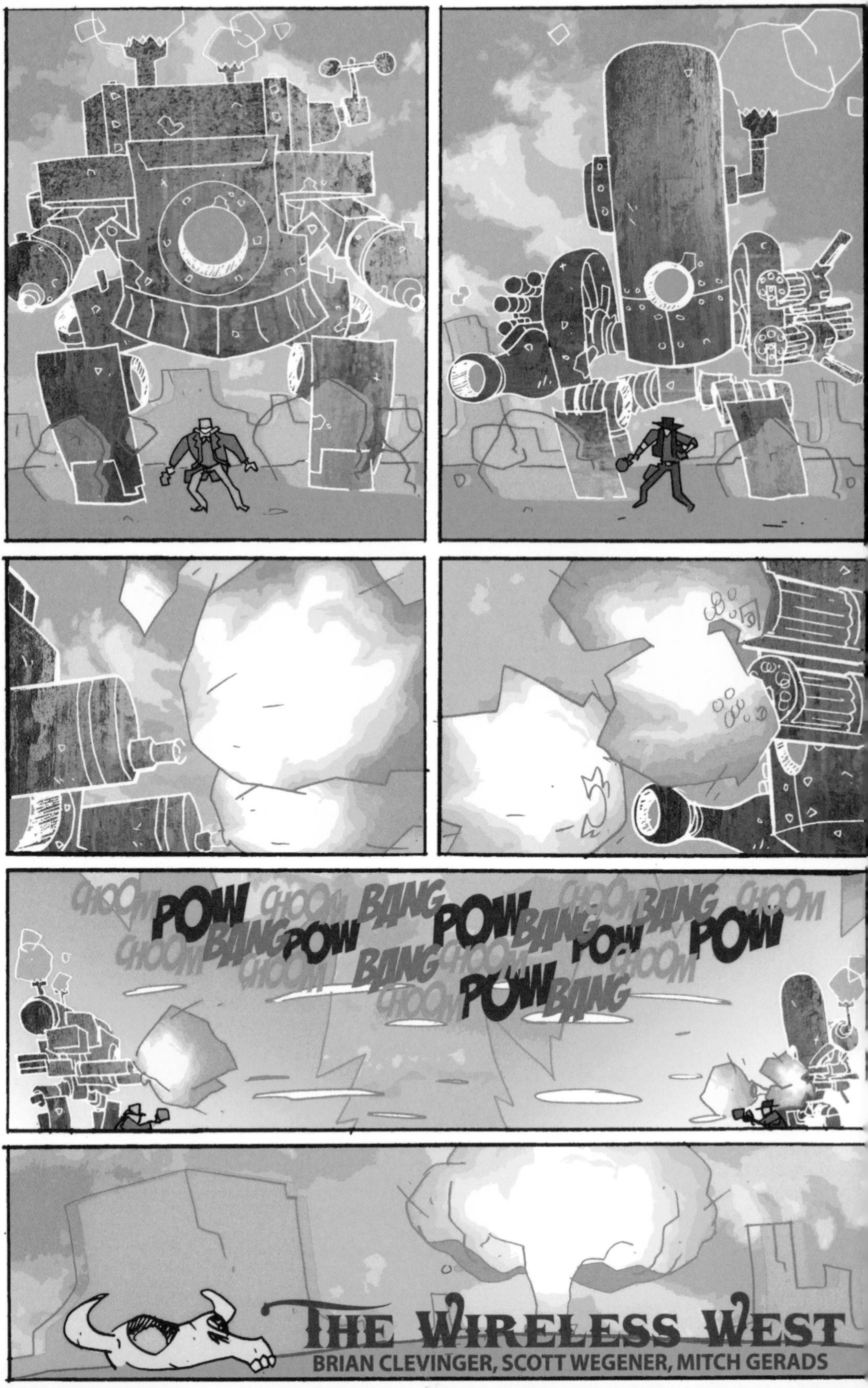
CHOOM POW CHOOM BANG
CHOOM BANG POW
CHOOM BANG
POW BANG CHOOM BANG CHOOM
BANG CHOOM POW CHOOM POW
CHOOM POW BANG
THE WIRELESS WEST
BRIAN CLEVINGER, SCOTT WEGENER, MITCH GERADS

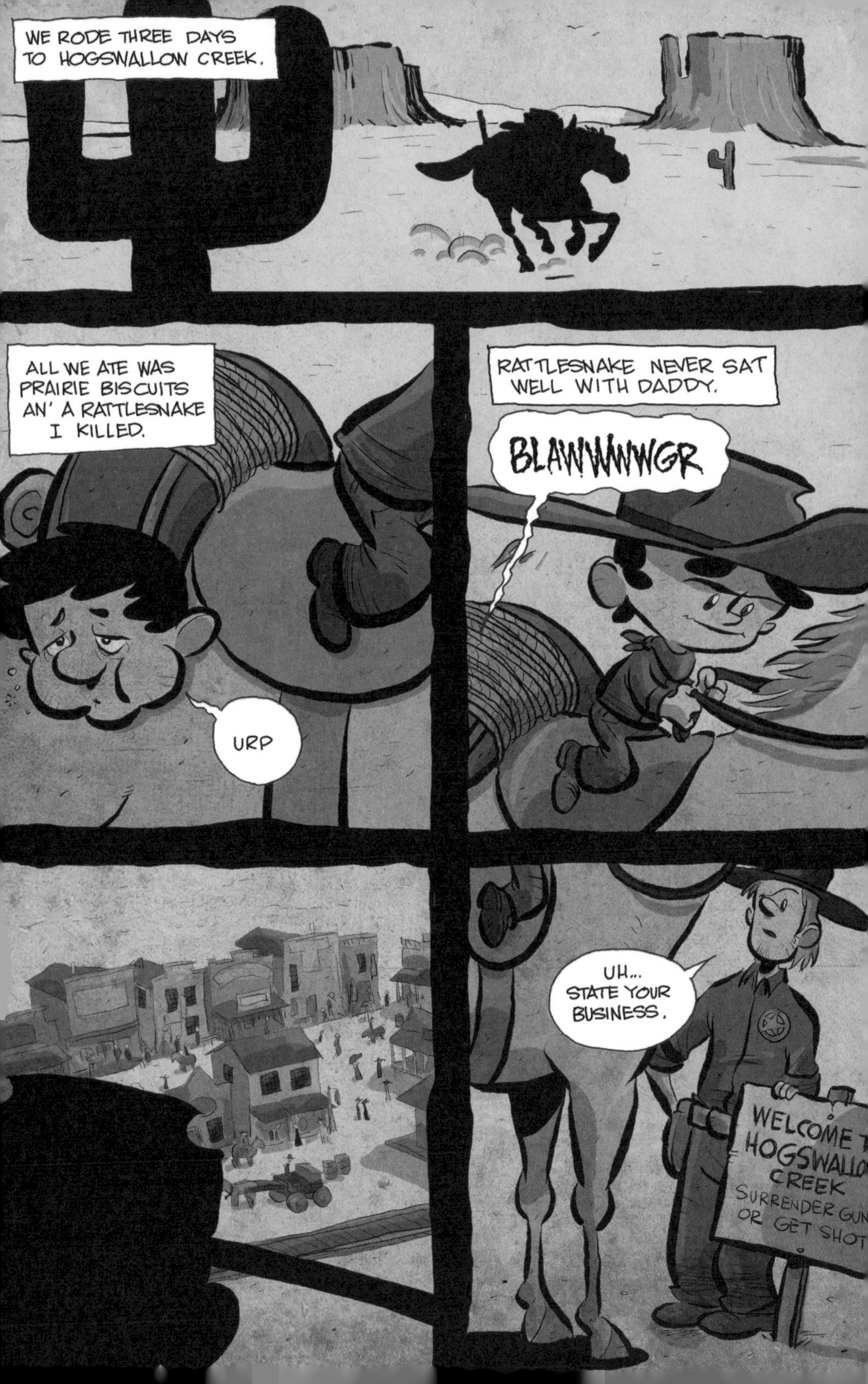
WE RODE THREE DAYS TO HOGSWALLOW CREEK.
ALL WE ATE WAS PRAIRIE BISCUITS AN' A RATTLESNAKE I KILLED.
URP
RATTLESNAKE NEVER SAT WELL WITH DADDY.
BLAWWWWGR
UH... STATE YOUR BUSINESS.
WELCOME T HOGSWALLO CREEK SURRENDER GUN OR GET SHOT

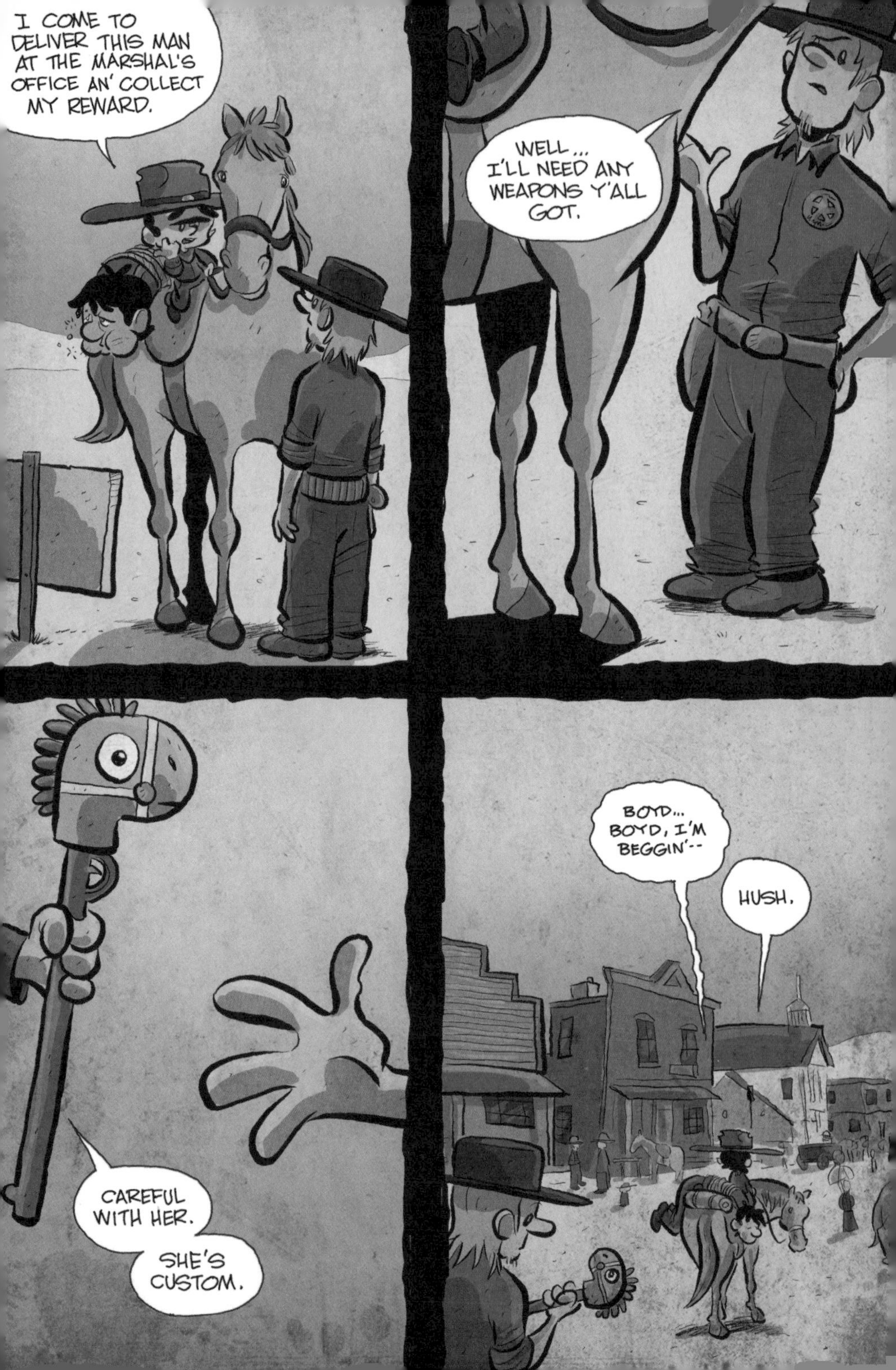
I COME TO DELIVER THIS MAN AT THE MARSHAL'S OFFICE AN' COLLECT MY REWARD.
WELL... I'LL NEED ANY WEAPONS Y'ALL GOT.
CAREFUL WITH HER.
SHE'S CUSTOM.
BOYD... BOYD, I'M BEGGIN'--
HUSH.

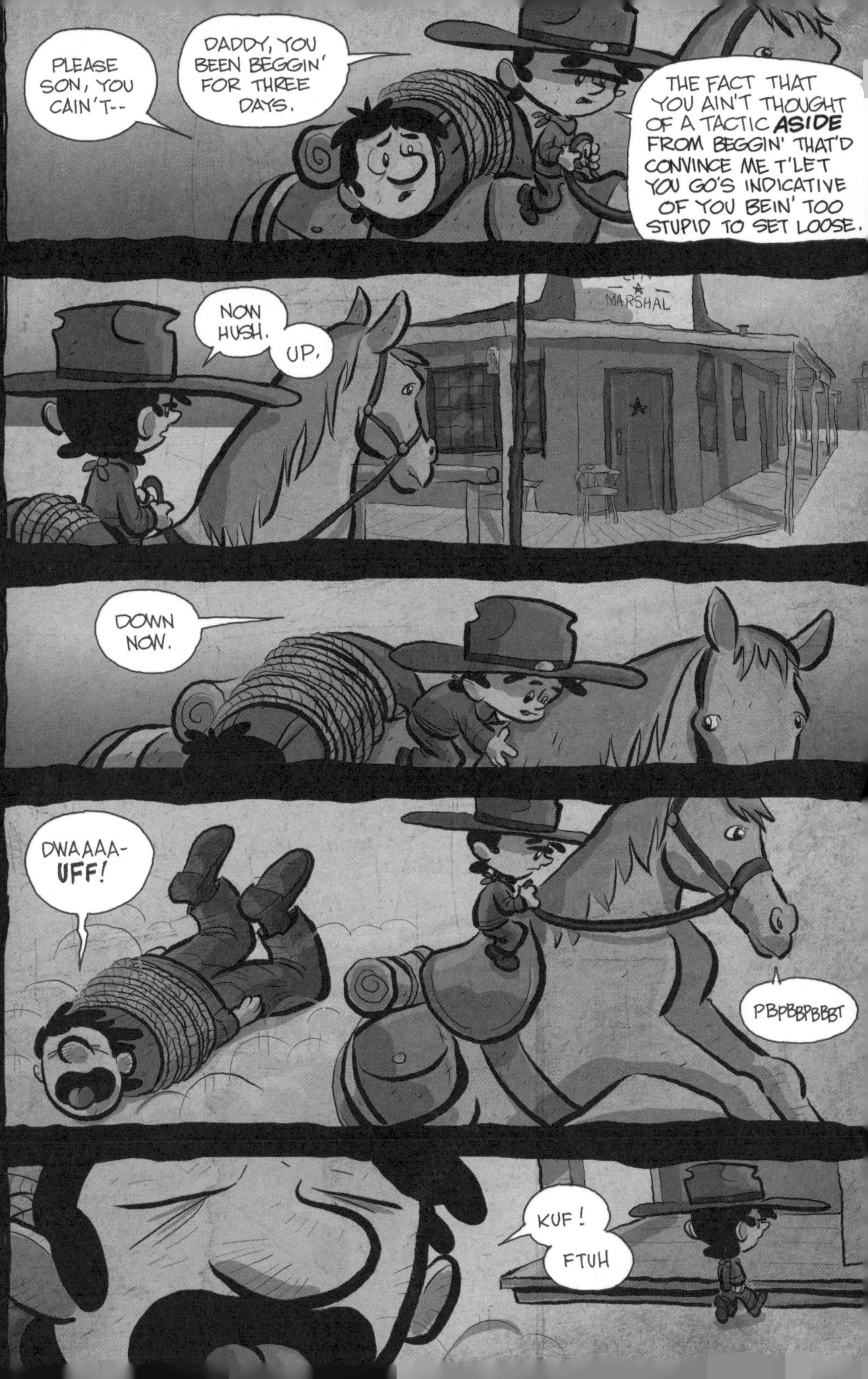
PLEASE SON, YOU CAIN'T--
DADDY, YOU BEEN BEGGIN' FOR THREE DAYS.
THE FACT THAT YOU AIN'T THOUGHT OF A TACTIC **ASIDE** FROM BEGGIN' THAT'D CONVINCE ME T'LET YOU GO'S INDICATIVE OF YOU BEIN' TOO STUPID TO SET LOOSE.
MARSHAL
NOW HUSH.
UP.
DOWN NOW.
DWAAAA-**UFF!**
PBPBBPBBBT
KUF!
FTUH

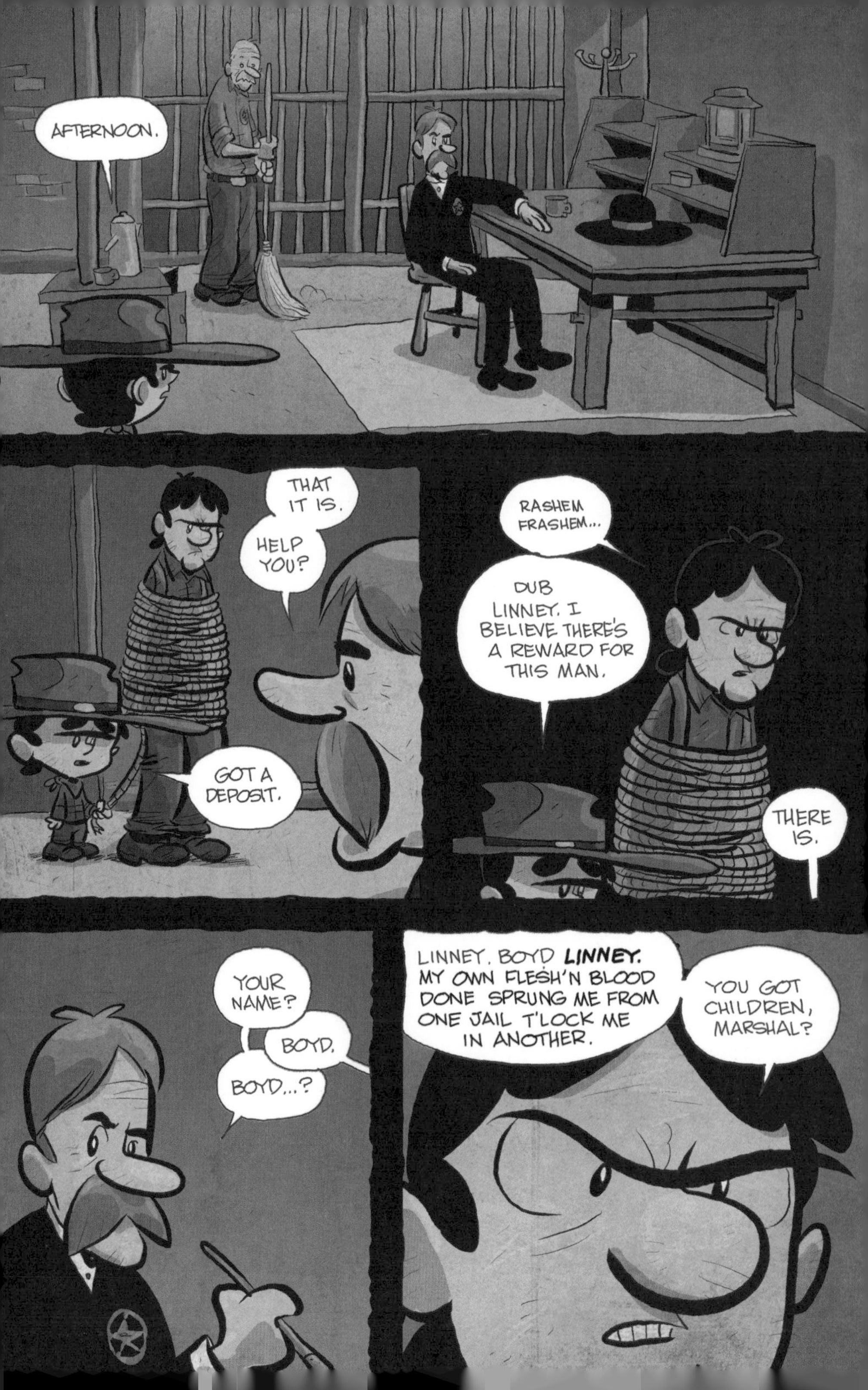
AFTERNOON.
THAT IT IS.
HELP YOU?
GOT A DEPOSIT.
RASHEM FRASHEM...
DUB LINNEY. I BELIEVE THERE'S A REWARD FOR THIS MAN.
THERE IS.
YOUR NAME?
BOYD.
BOYD...?
LINNEY. BOYD **LINNEY.** MY OWN FLESH'N BLOOD DONE SPRUNG ME FROM ONE JAIL T'LOCK ME IN ANOTHER.
YOU GOT CHILDREN, MARSHAL?

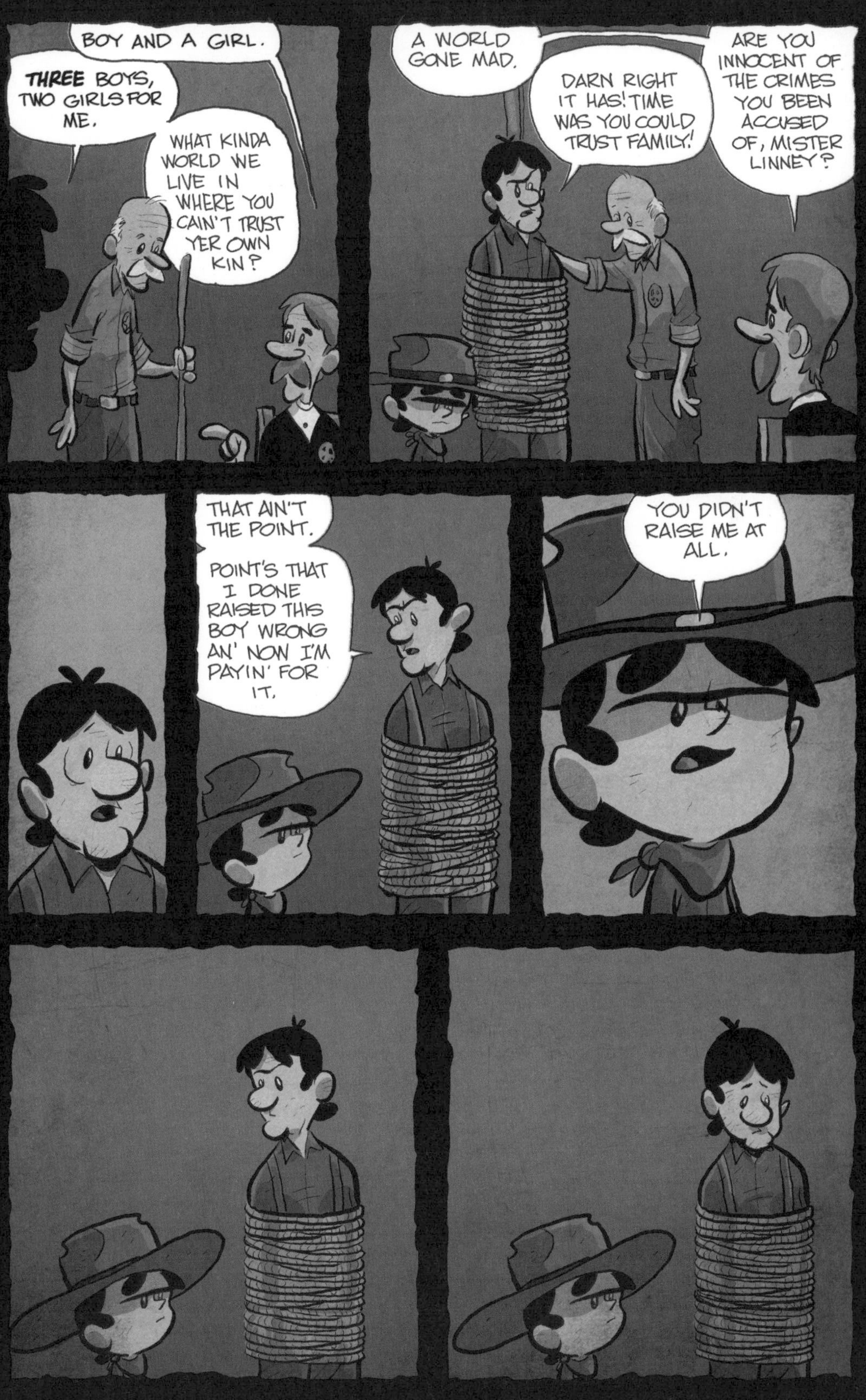
BOY AND A GIRL.
THREE BOYS, TWO GIRLS FOR ME.
WHAT KINDA WORLD WE LIVE IN WHERE YOU CAIN'T TRUST YER OWN KIN?
A WORLD GONE MAD.
DARN RIGHT IT HAS! TIME WAS YOU COULD TRUST FAMILY!
ARE YOU INNOCENT OF THE CRIMES YOU BEEN ACCUSED OF, MISTER LINNEY?
THAT AIN'T THE POINT.
POINT'S THAT I DONE RAISED THIS BOY WRONG AN' NOW I'M PAYIN' FOR IT.
YOU DIDN'T RAISE ME AT ALL.

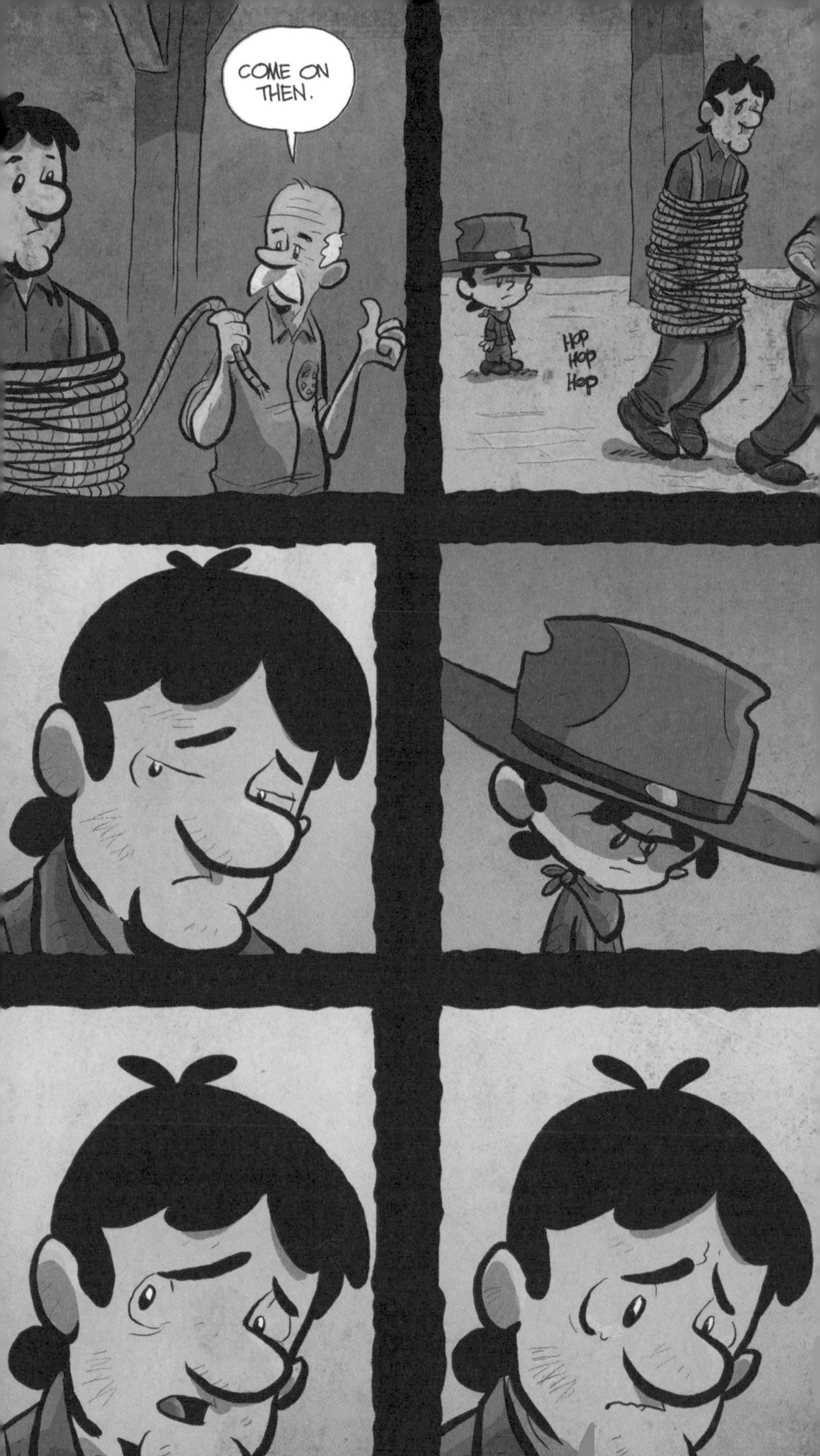
COME ON THEN.
HOP HOP HOP

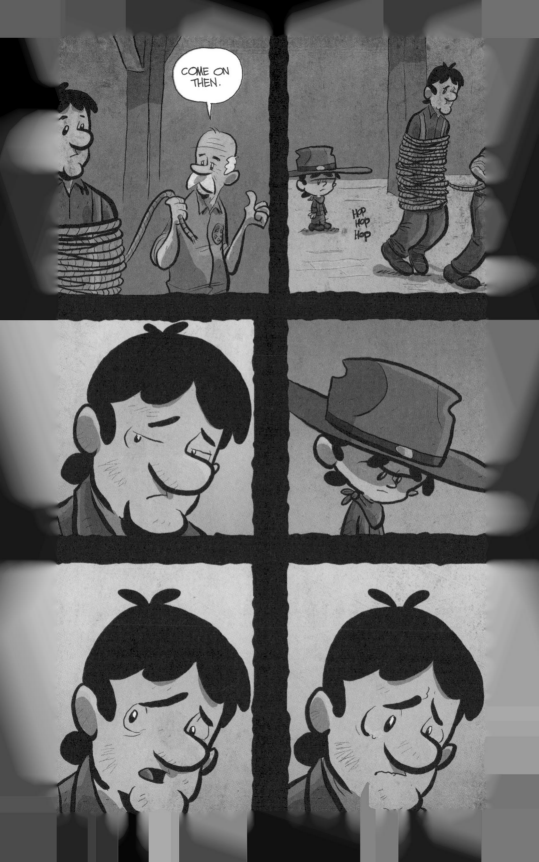

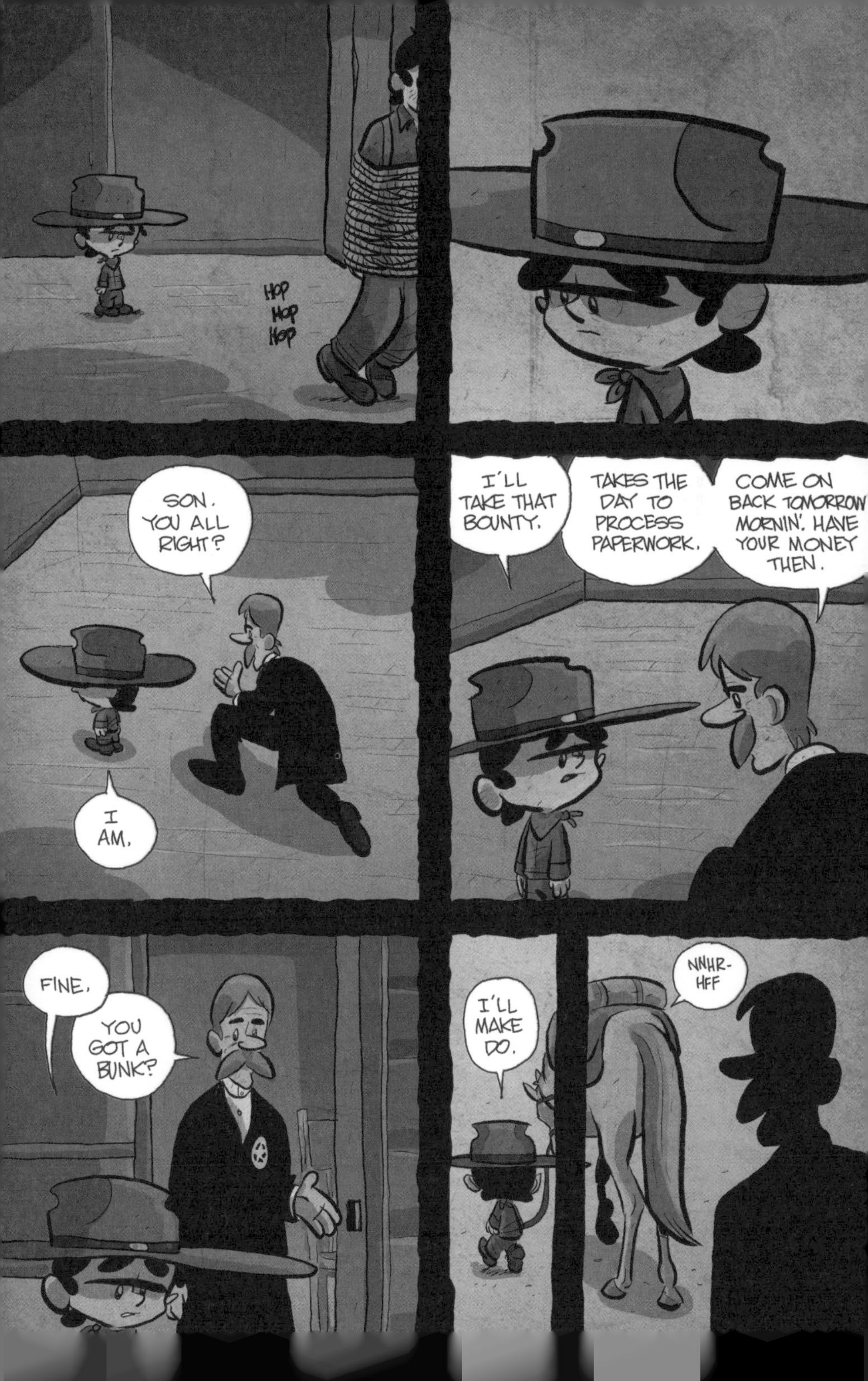
HOP
HOP
HOP
SON. YOU ALL RIGHT?
I AM.
I'LL TAKE THAT BOUNTY.
TAKES THE DAY TO PROCESS PAPERWORK.
COME ON BACK TOMORROW MORNIN'. HAVE YOUR MONEY THEN.
FINE.
YOU GOT A BUNK?
I'LL MAKE DO.
NNHR-HFF

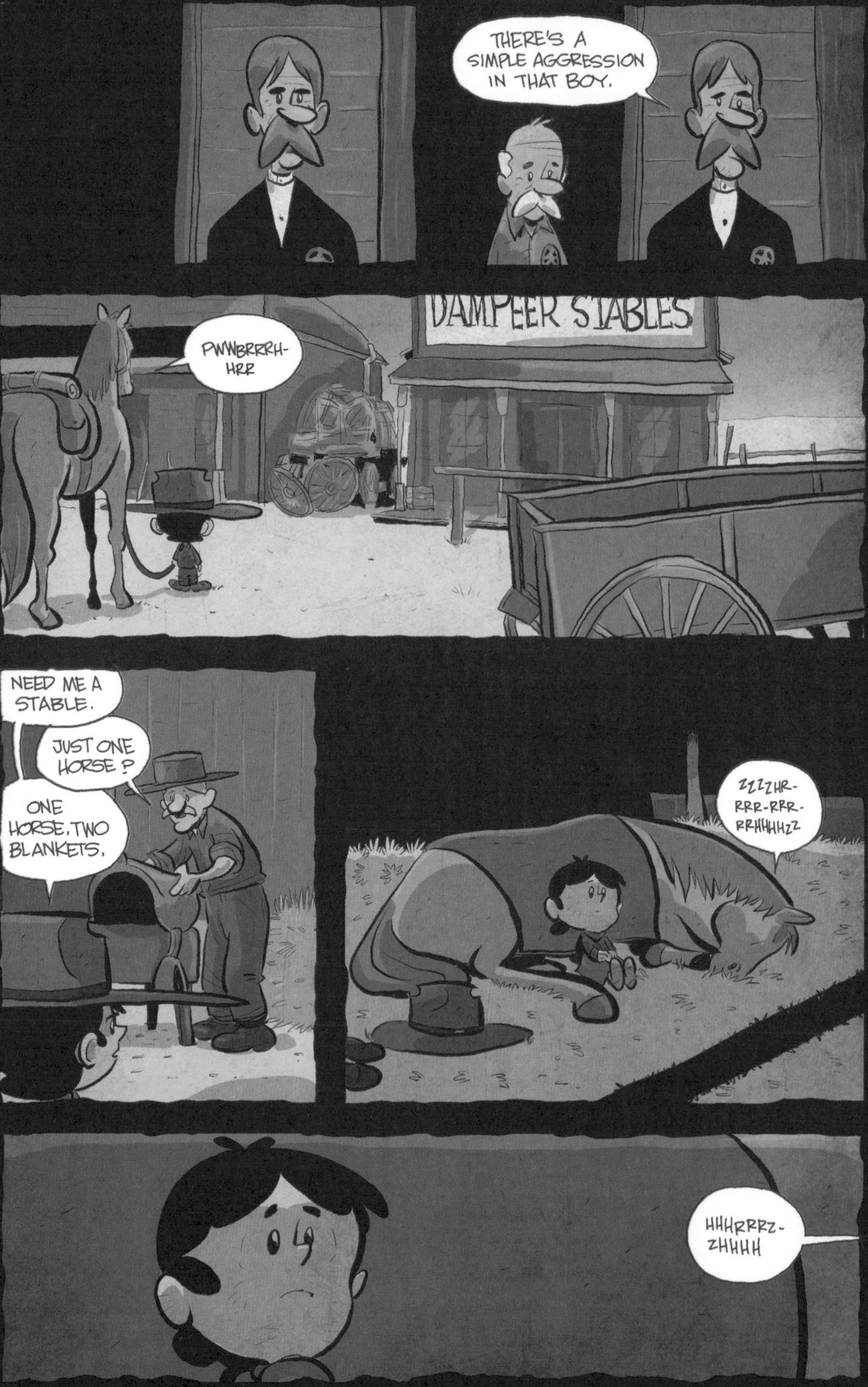
THERE'S A SIMPLE AGGRESSION IN THAT BOY.
DAMPEER STABLES
PWWBRRRH-HRR
NEED ME A STABLE.
JUST ONE HORSE ?
ONE HORSE, TWO BLANKETS.
ZZZZHR-RRR-RRR-RRHHHHZZ
HHHRRRZ-ZHHHH

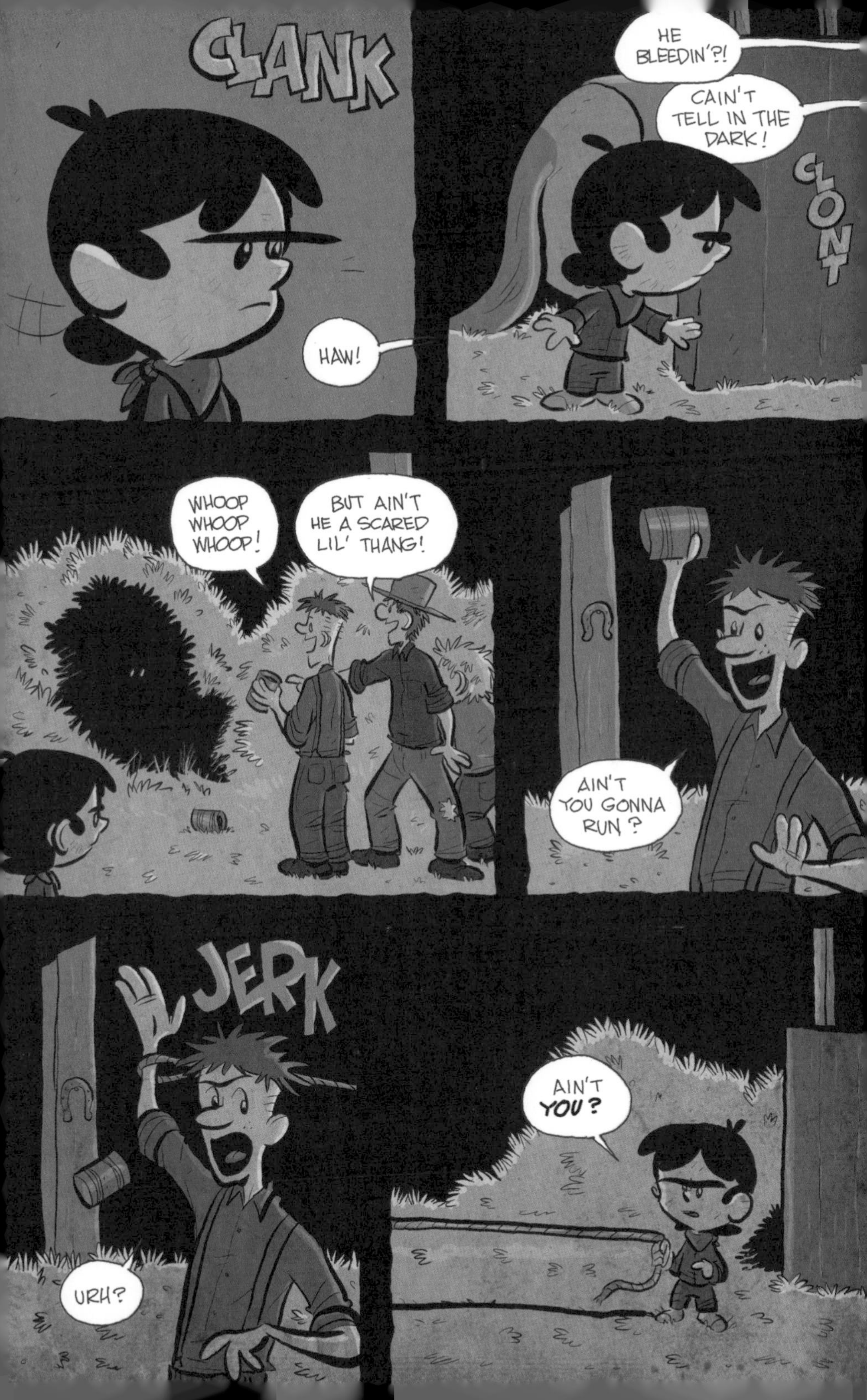
CLANK
HAW!
HE BLEEDIN'?!
CAIN'T TELL IN THE DARK!
CLONT
WHOOP WHOOP WHOOP!
BUT AIN'T HE A SCARED LIL' THANG!
AIN'T YOU GONNA RUN ?
JERK
URH?
AIN'T *YOU*?

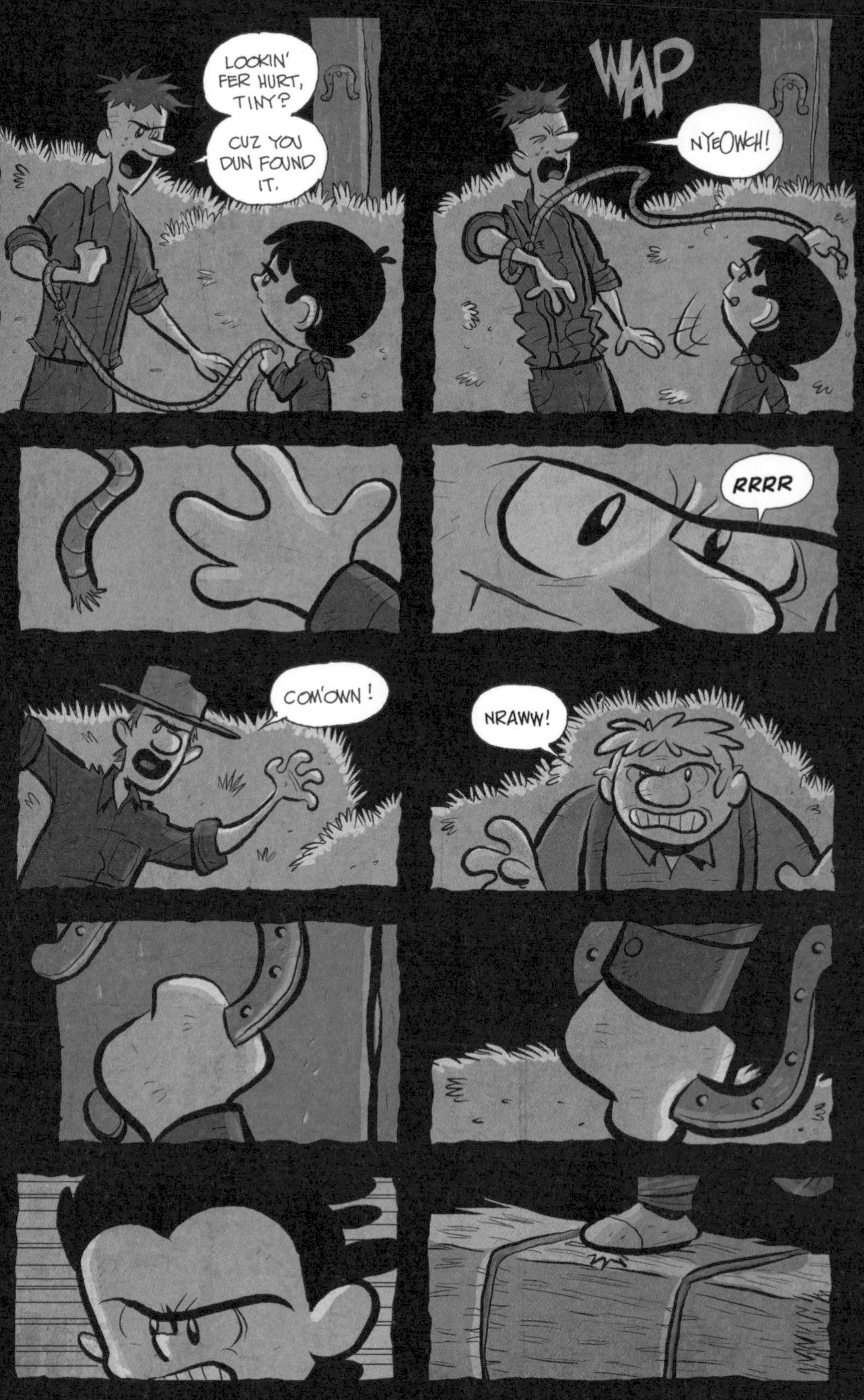
LOOKIN' FER HURT, TINY?
CUZ YOU DUN FOUND IT.
WAP
NYEOWCH!
RRRR
COM'OWN!
NRAWW!

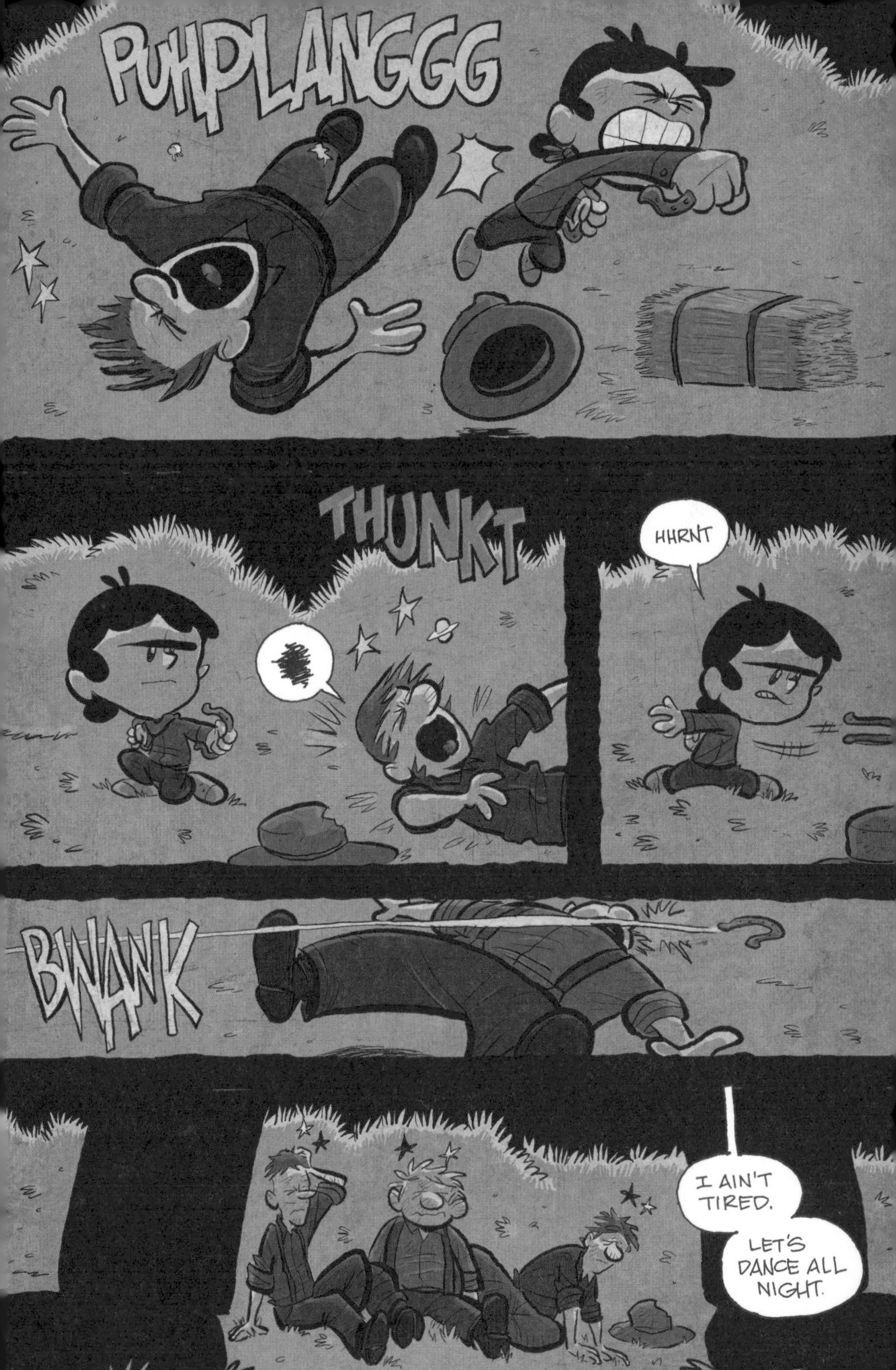
PUHPLANGGG
THUNKT
HHRNT
BWANK
I AIN'T TIRED.
LET'S DANCE ALL NIGHT.

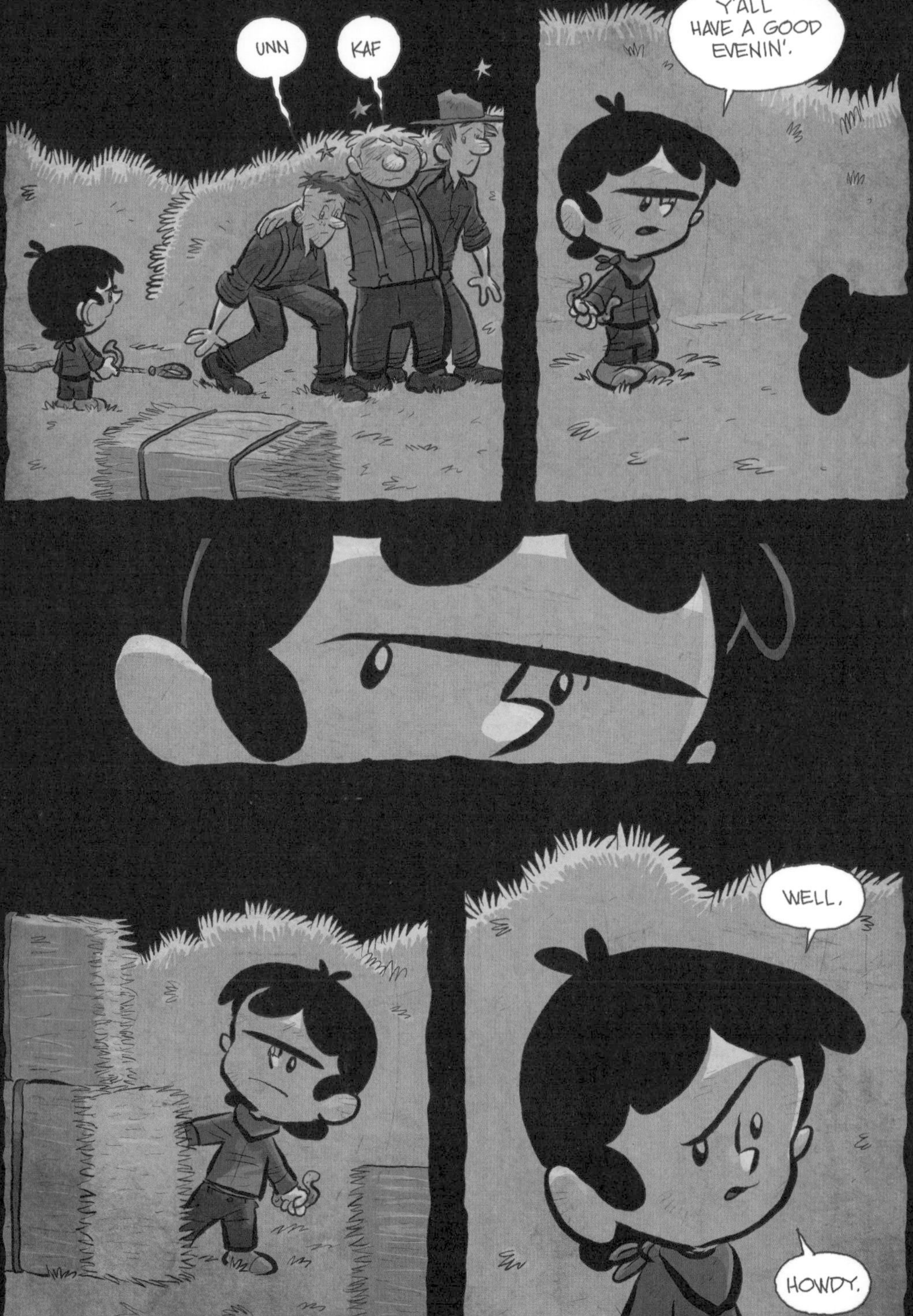
UNN
KAF
Y'ALL HAVE A GOOD EVENIN'.
WELL.
HOWDY.

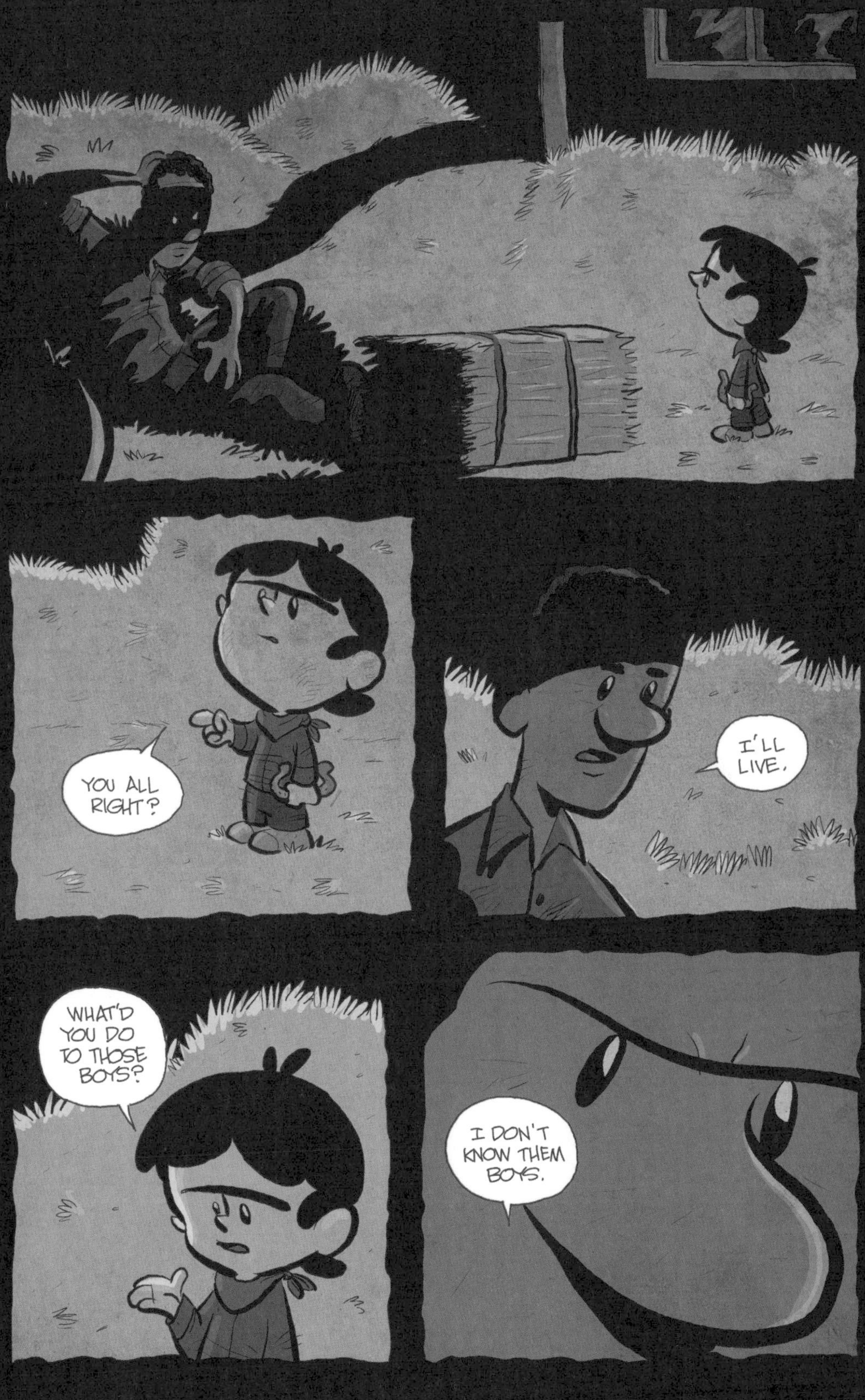
YOU ALL RIGHT?
I'LL LIVE.
WHAT'D YOU DO TO THOSE BOYS?
I DON'T KNOW THEM BOYS.

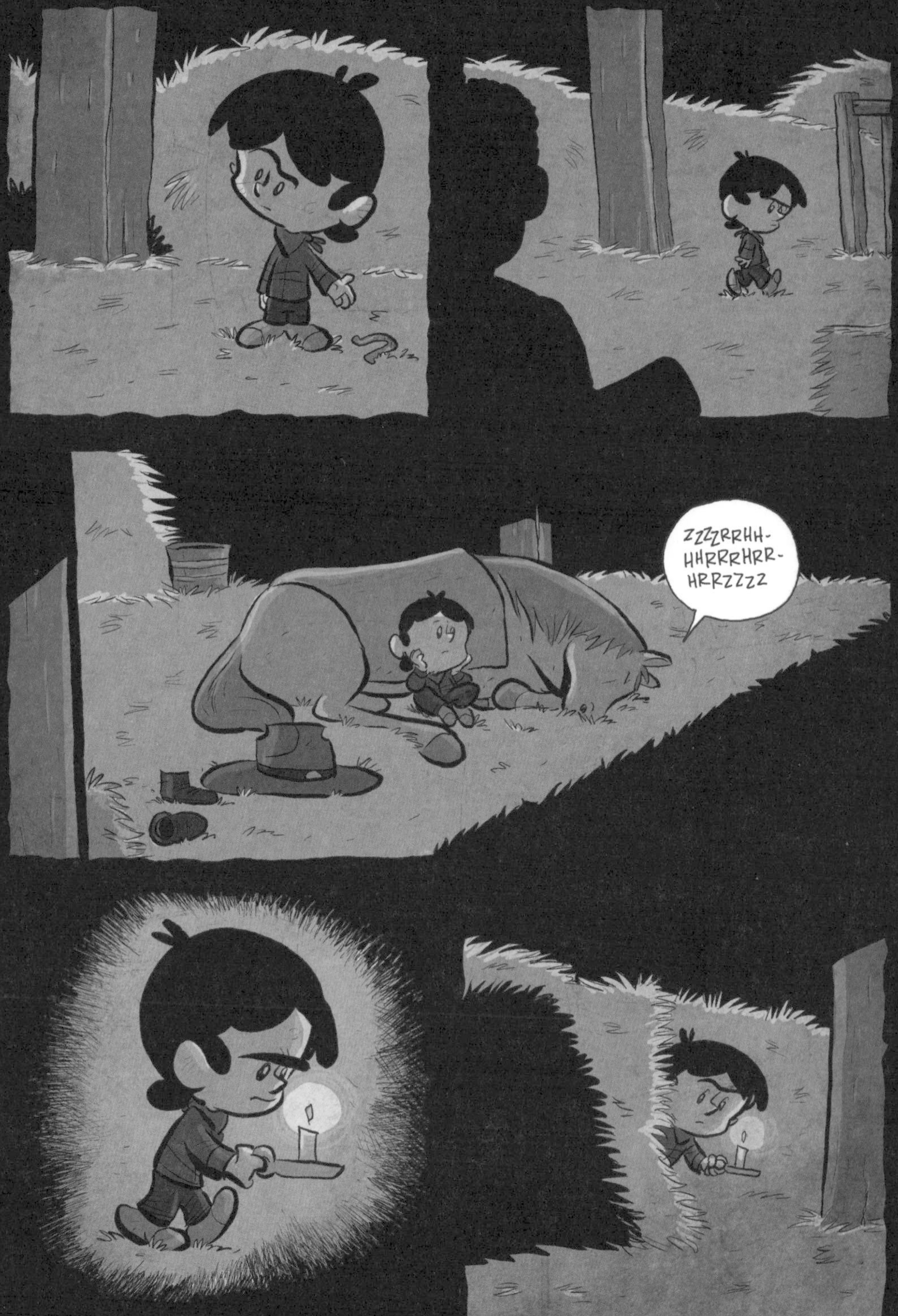
ZZZZRRHH-
HHRRRHRR-
HRRZZZZ

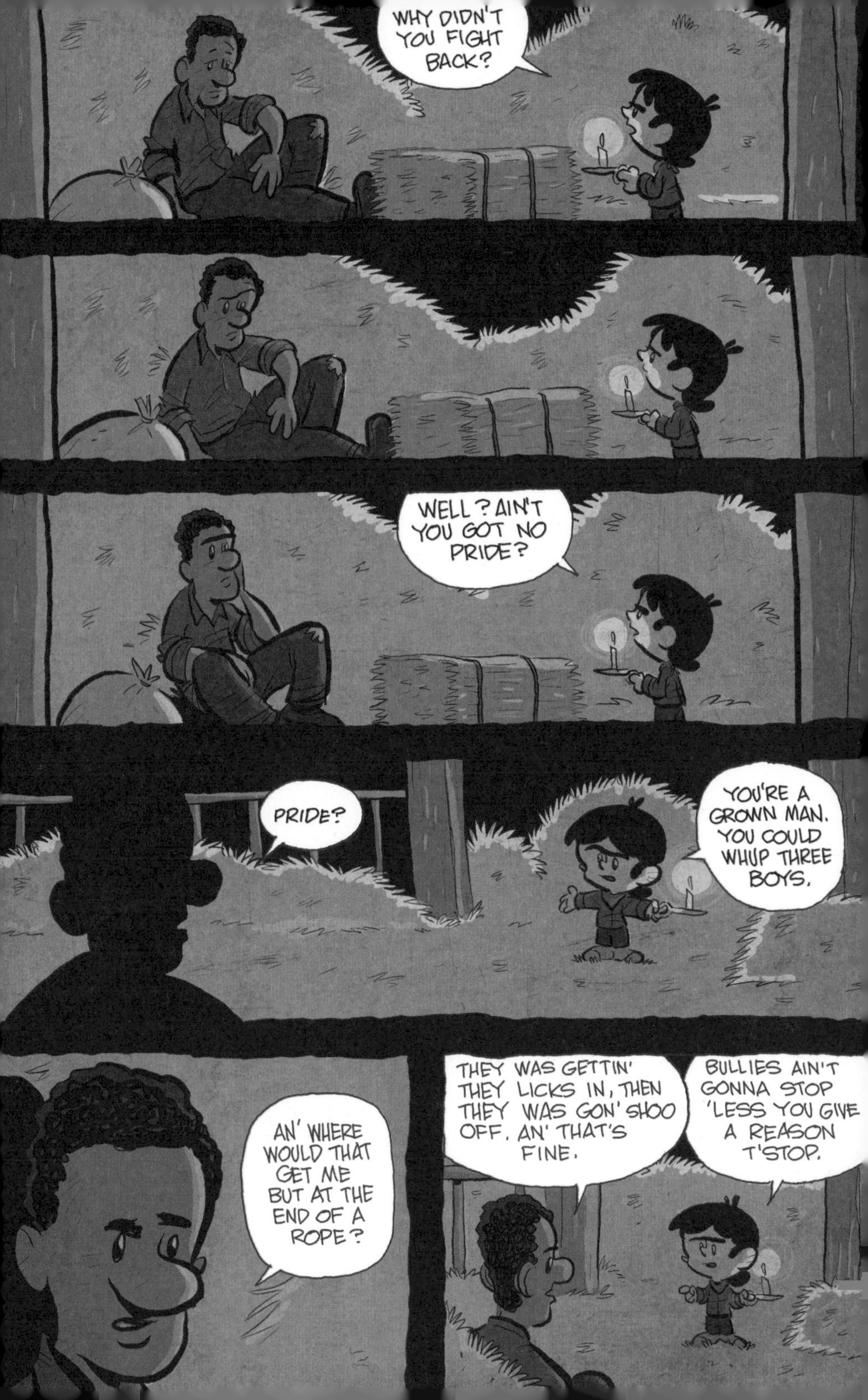
WHY DIDN'T YOU FIGHT BACK?
WELL? AIN'T YOU GOT NO PRIDE?
PRIDE?
YOU'RE A GROWN MAN. YOU COULD WHUP THREE BOYS.
AN' WHERE WOULD THAT GET ME BUT AT THE END OF A ROPE?
THEY WAS GETTIN' THEY LICKS IN, THEN THEY WAS GON' SHOO OFF. AN' THAT'S FINE.
BULLIES AIN'T GONNA STOP 'LESS YOU GIVE A REASON T'STOP.

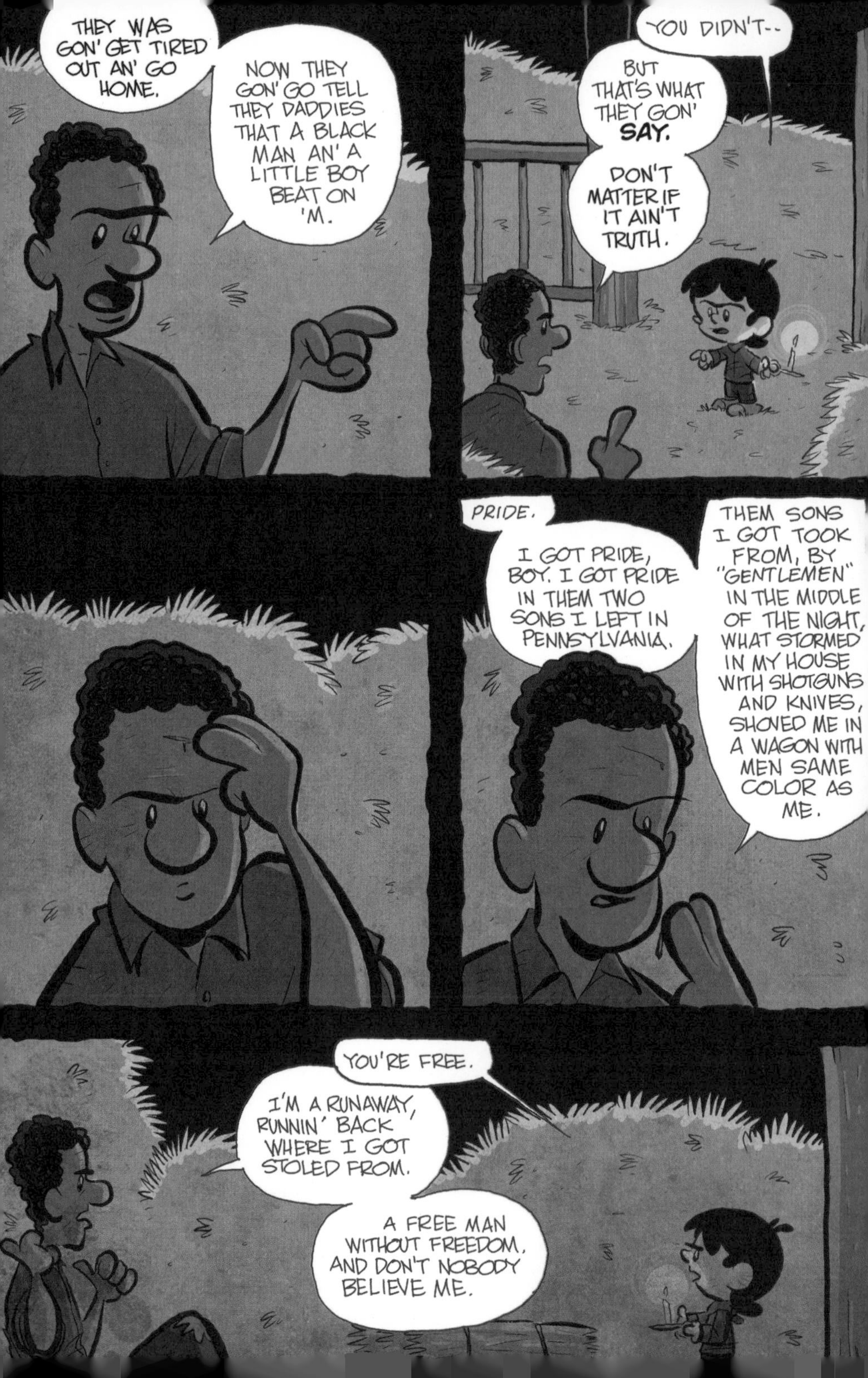
THEY WAS GON' GET TIRED OUT AN' GO HOME.
NOW THEY GON' GO TELL THEY DADDIES THAT A BLACK MAN AN' A LITTLE BOY BEAT ON 'M.
YOU DIDN'T--
BUT THAT'S WHAT THEY GON' SAY.
DON'T MATTER IF IT AIN'T TRUTH.
PRIDE.
I GOT PRIDE, BOY. I GOT PRIDE IN THEM TWO SONS I LEFT IN PENNSYLVANIA.
THEM SONS I GOT TOOK FROM, BY "GENTLEMEN" IN THE MIDDLE OF THE NIGHT, WHAT STORMED IN MY HOUSE WITH SHOTGUNS AND KNIVES, SHOVED ME IN A WAGON WITH MEN SAME COLOR AS ME.
YOU'RE FREE.
I'M A RUNAWAY, RUNNIN' BACK WHERE I GOT STOLED FROM.
A FREE MAN WITHOUT FREEDOM, AND DON'T NOBODY BELIEVE ME.

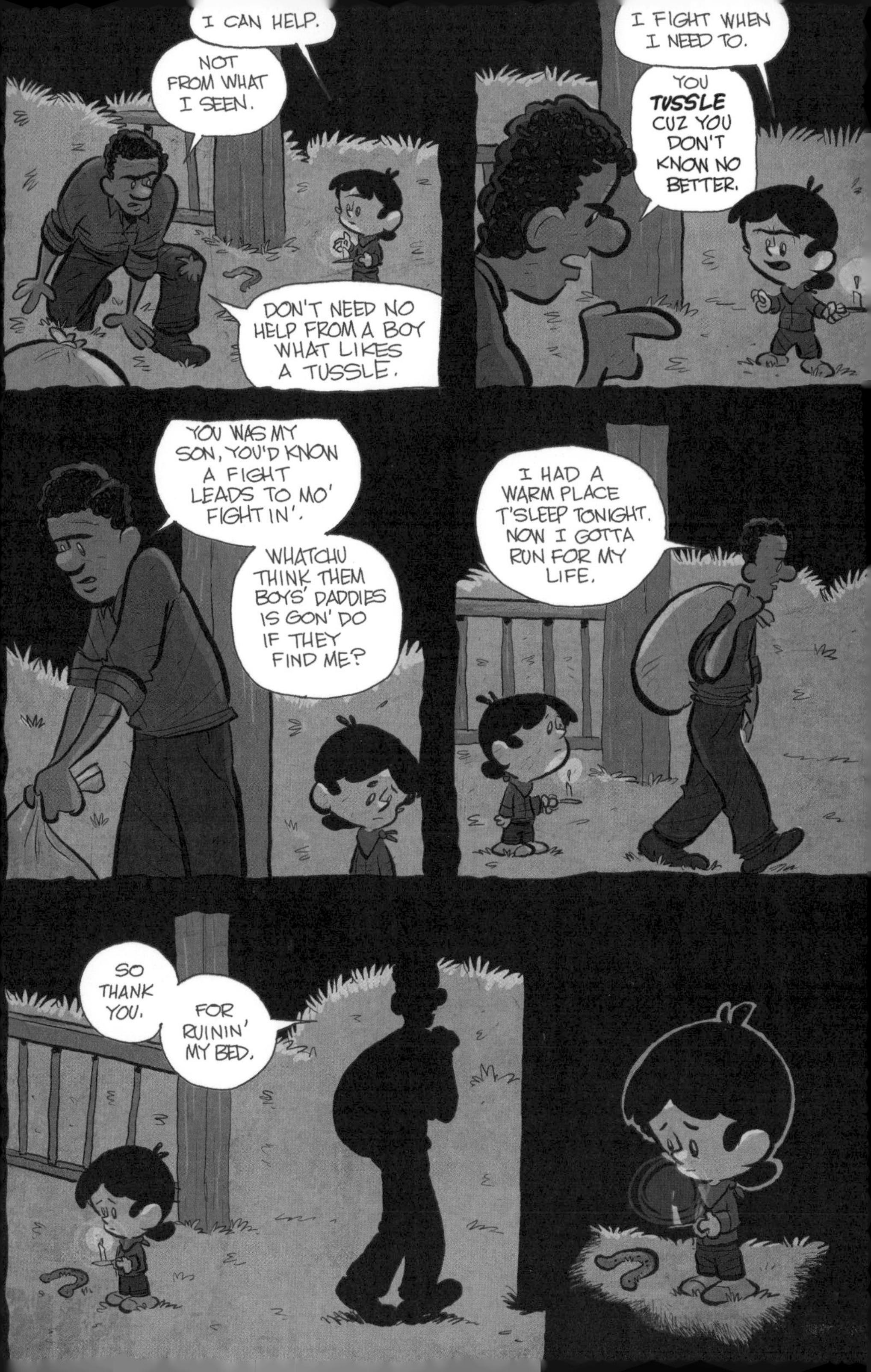
I CAN HELP.
NOT FROM WHAT I SEEN.
DON'T NEED NO HELP FROM A BOY WHAT LIKES A TUSSLE.
I FIGHT WHEN I NEED TO.
YOU **TUSSLE** CUZ YOU DON'T KNOW NO BETTER.
YOU WAS MY SON, YOU'D KNOW A FIGHT LEADS TO MO' FIGHTIN'.
WHATCHU THINK THEM BOYS' DADDIES IS GON' DO IF THEY FIND ME?
I HAD A WARM PLACE T'SLEEP TONIGHT. NOW I GOTTA RUN FOR MY LIFE.
SO THANK YOU.
FOR RUININ' MY BED.

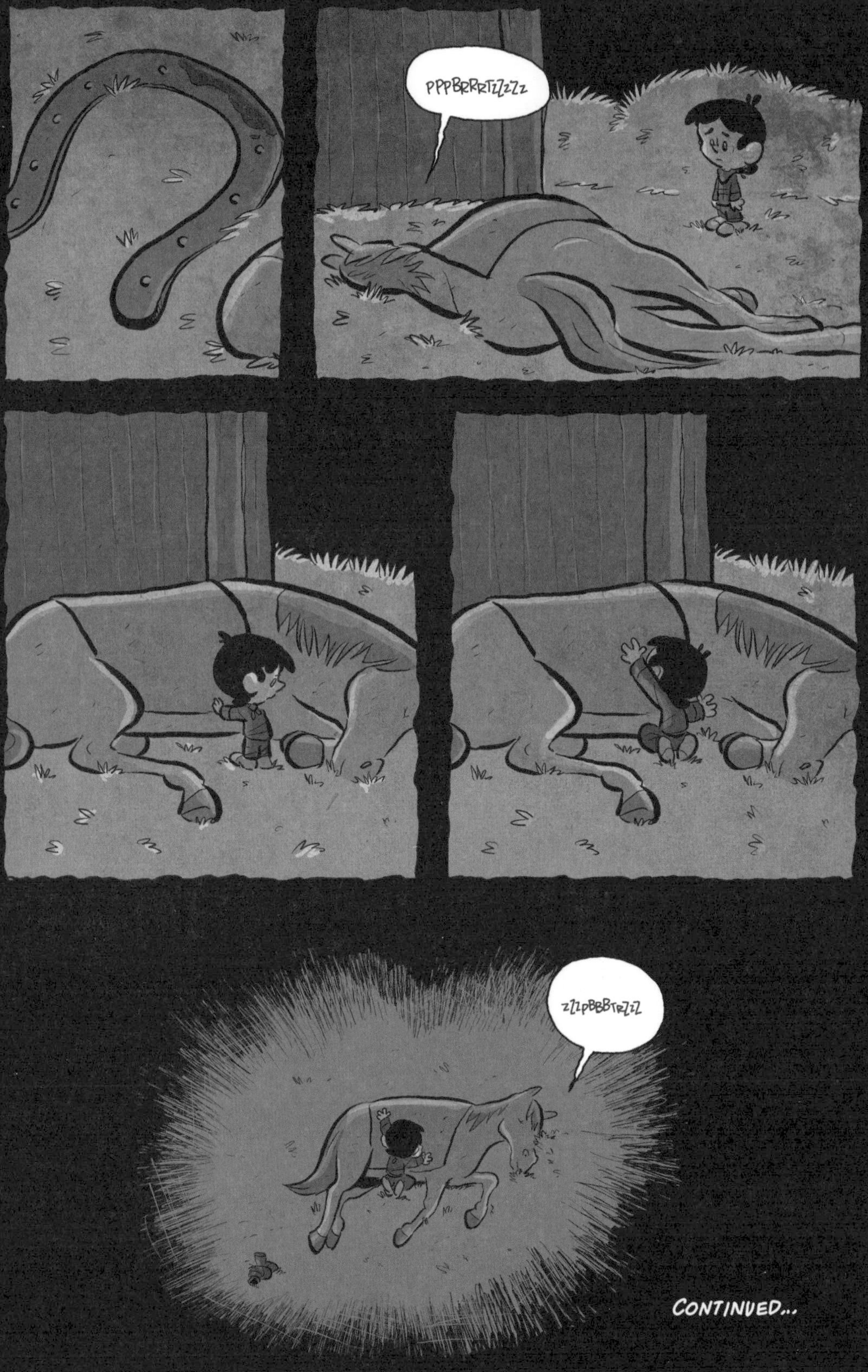
PPPBRRRTZZZZz
ZZZPBBBTRZZZ
CONTINUED...

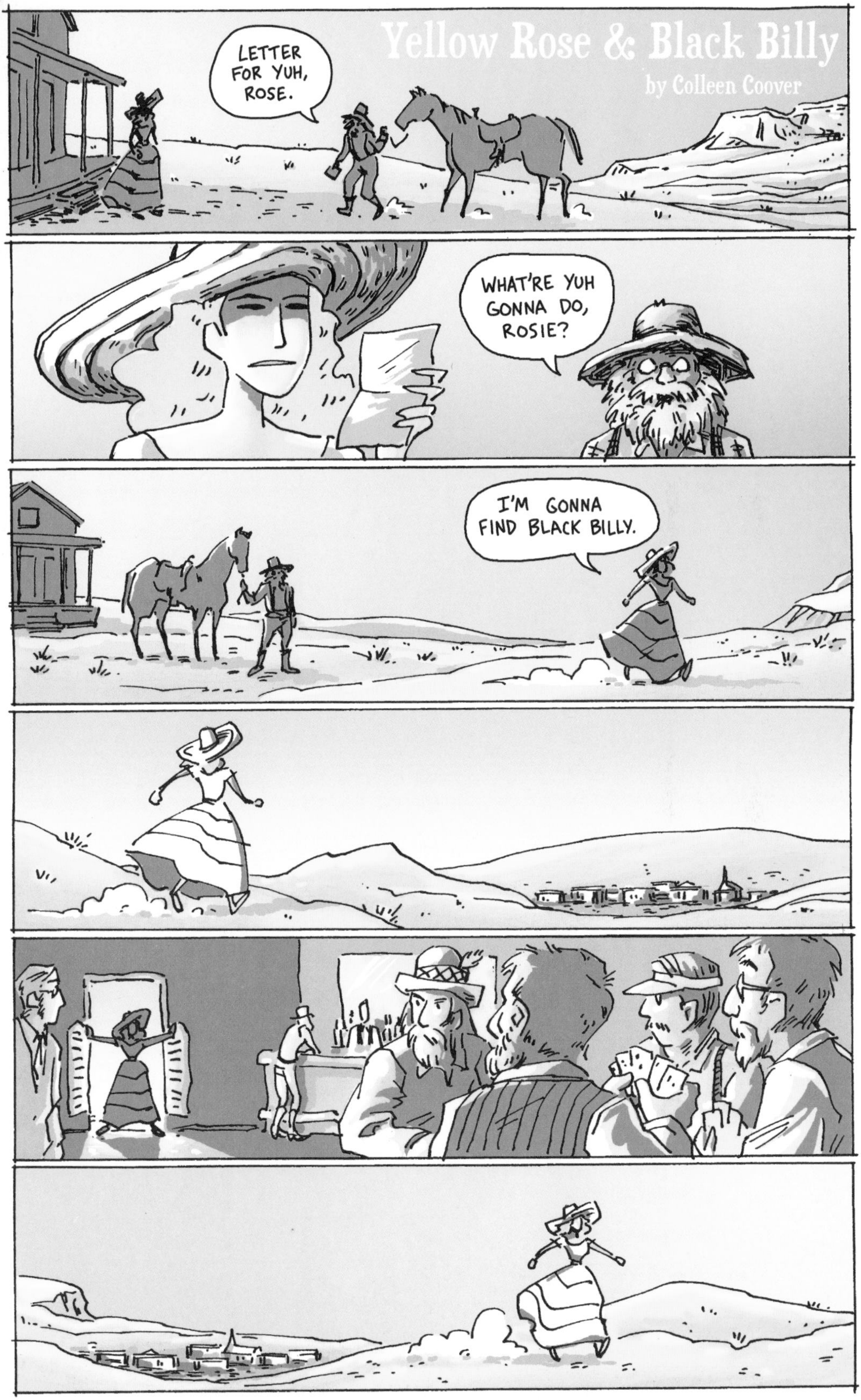
Yellow Rose & Black Billy
by Colleen Coover
LETTER FOR YUH, ROSE.
WHAT'RE YUH GONNA DO, ROSIE?
I'M GONNA FIND BLACK BILLY.

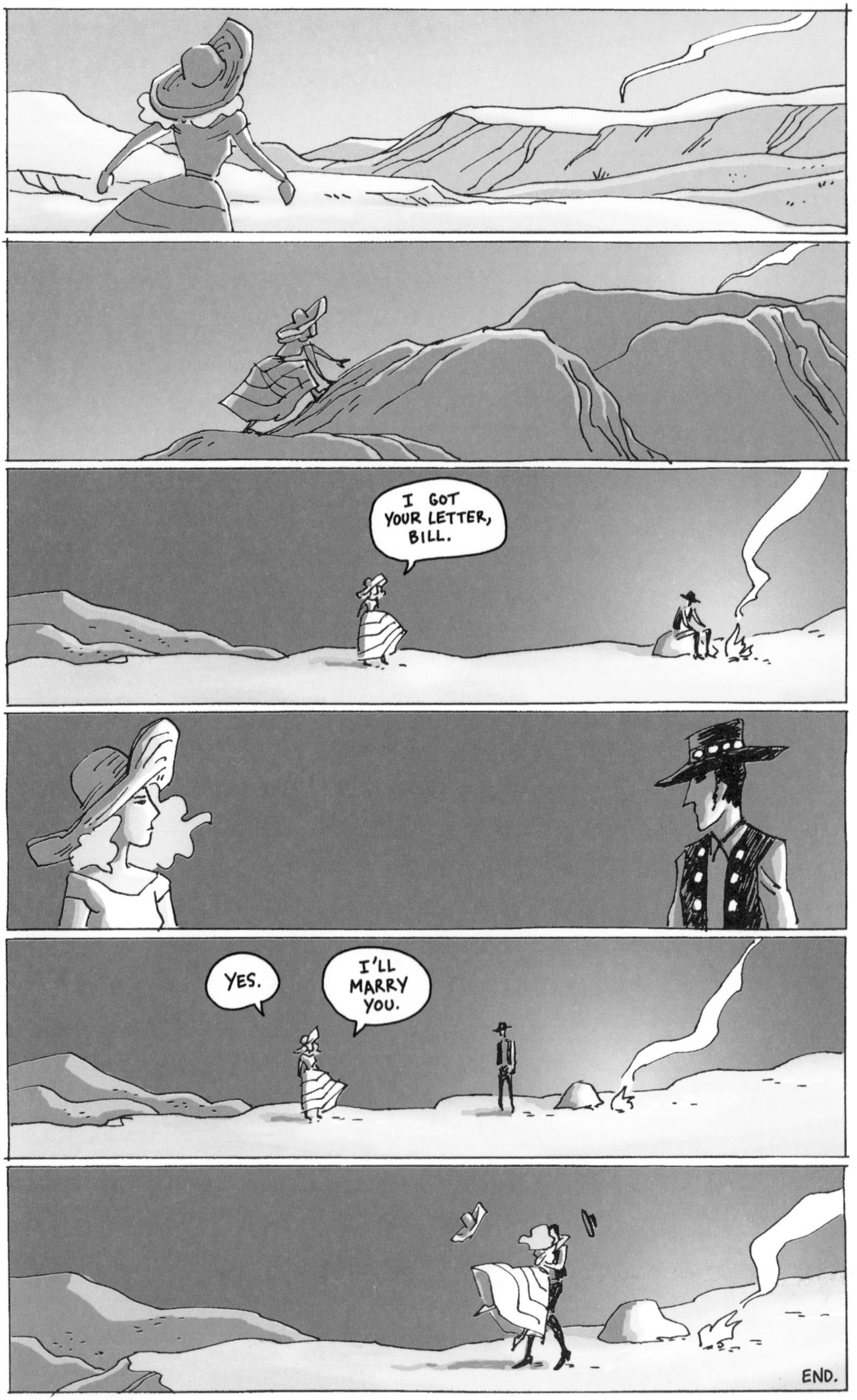
I GOT YOUR LETTER, BILL.
YES.
I'LL MARRY YOU.
END.

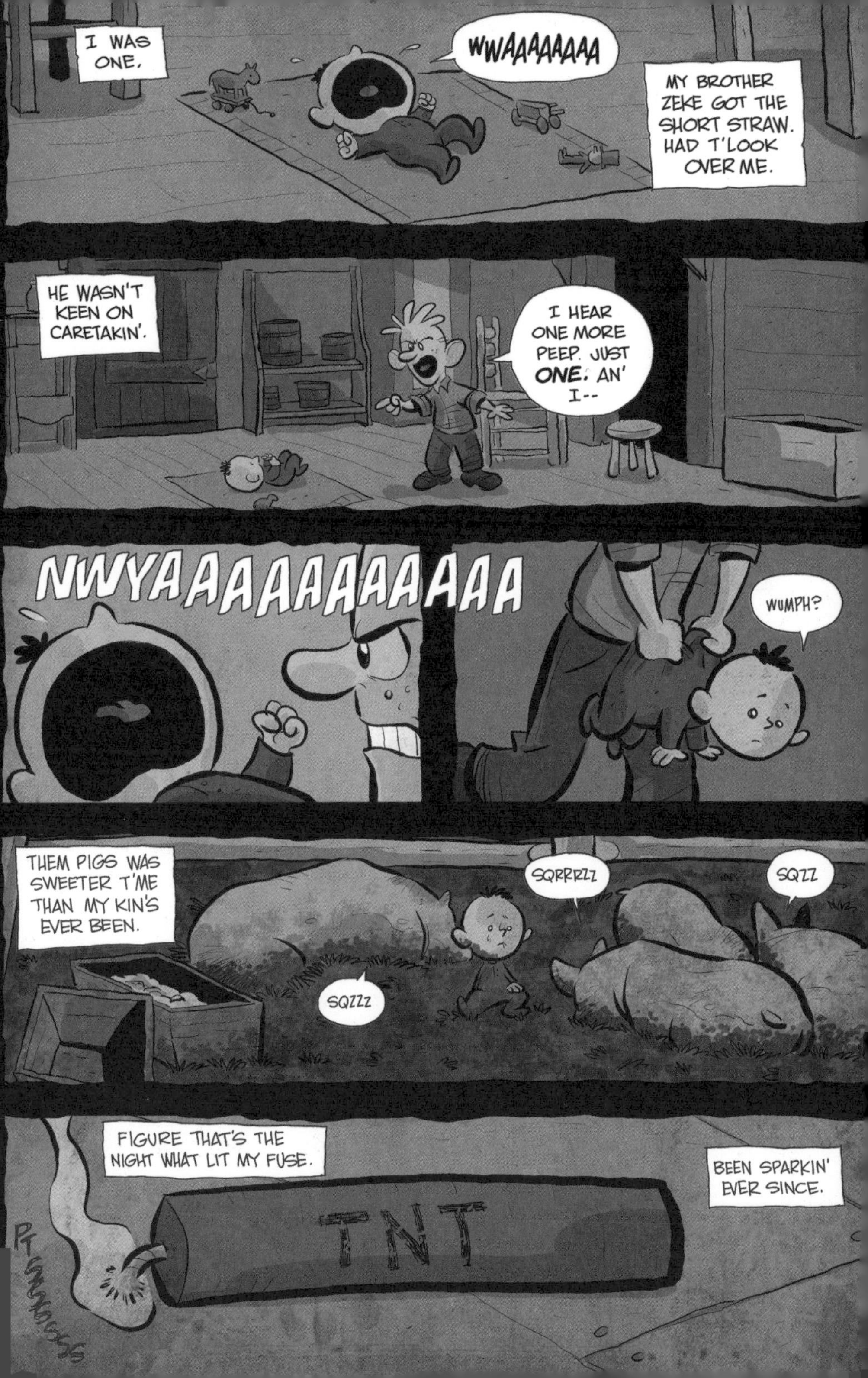
I WAS ONE.
WWAAAAAAAA
MY BROTHER ZEKE GOT THE SHORT STRAW. HAD T'LOOK OVER ME.
HE WASN'T KEEN ON CARETAKIN'.
I HEAR ONE MORE PEEP. JUST ONE: AN' I--
NWYAAAAAAAAAAA
WUMPH?
THEM PIGS WAS SWEETER T'ME THAN MY KIN'S EVER BEEN.
SQRRRZZZ
SQZZ
SQZZZ
FIGURE THAT'S THE NIGHT WHAT LIT MY FUSE.
BEEN SPARKIN' EVER SINCE.
TNT

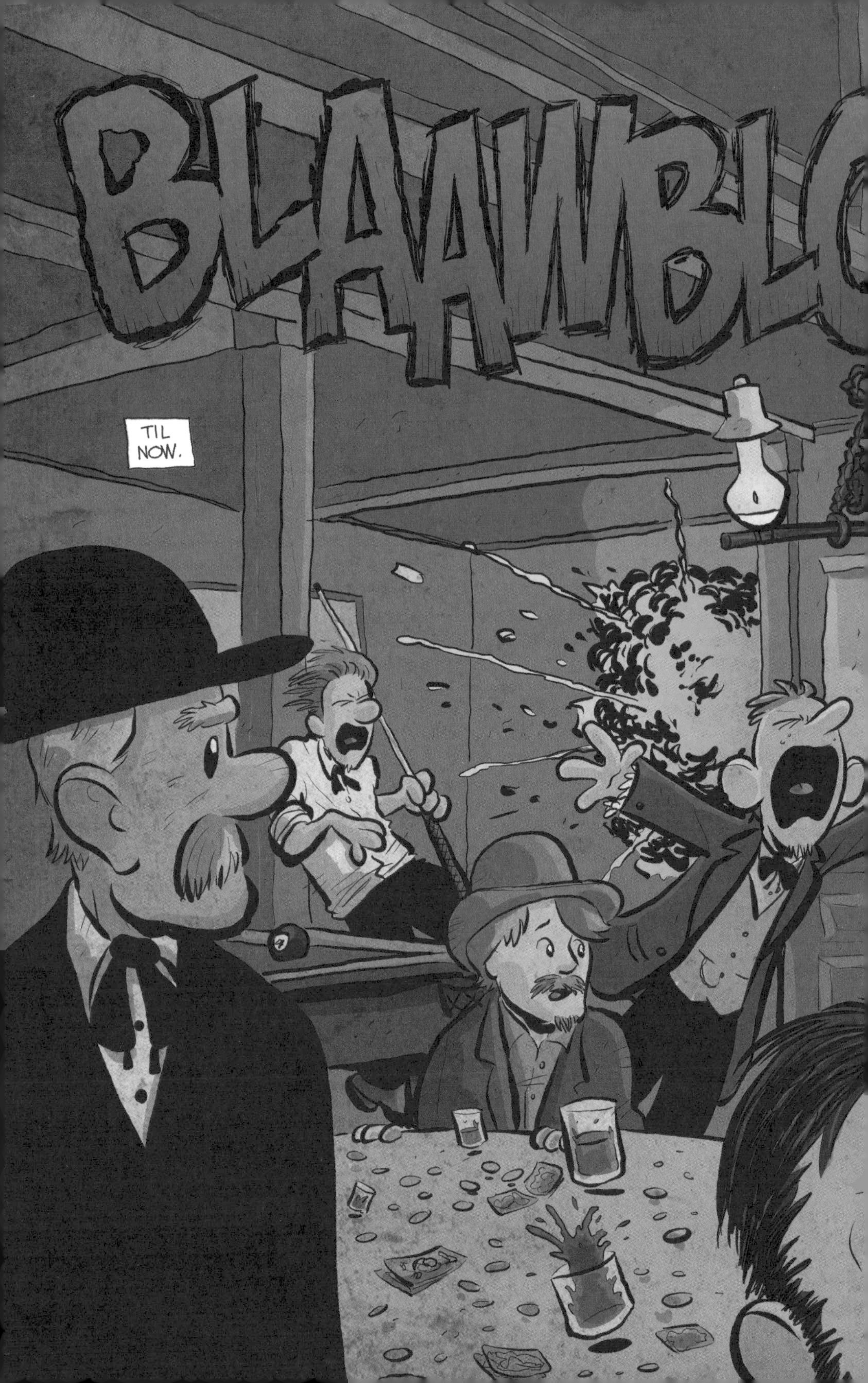
BLAAWBLO
TIL NOW.

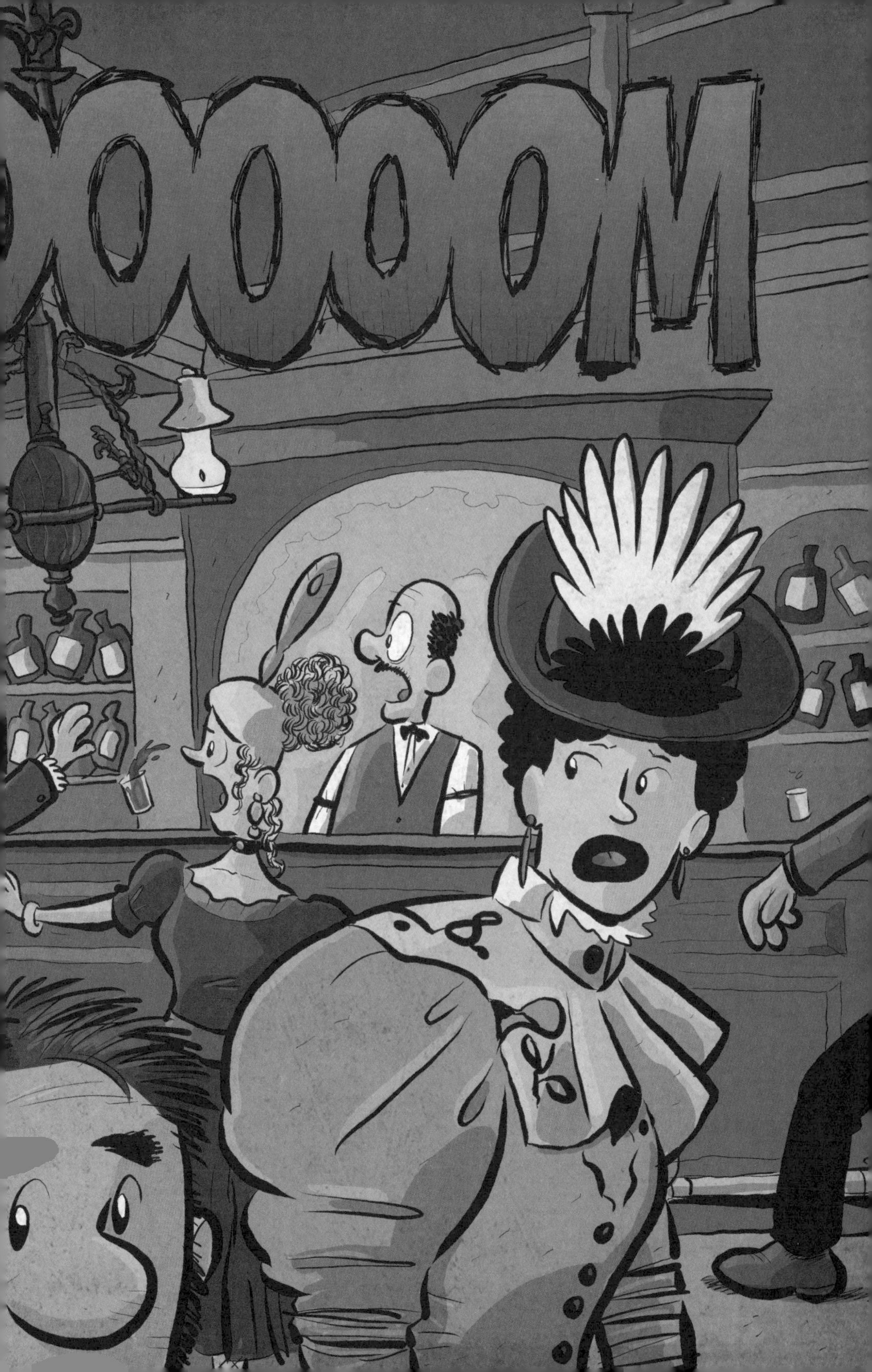
OOOOM

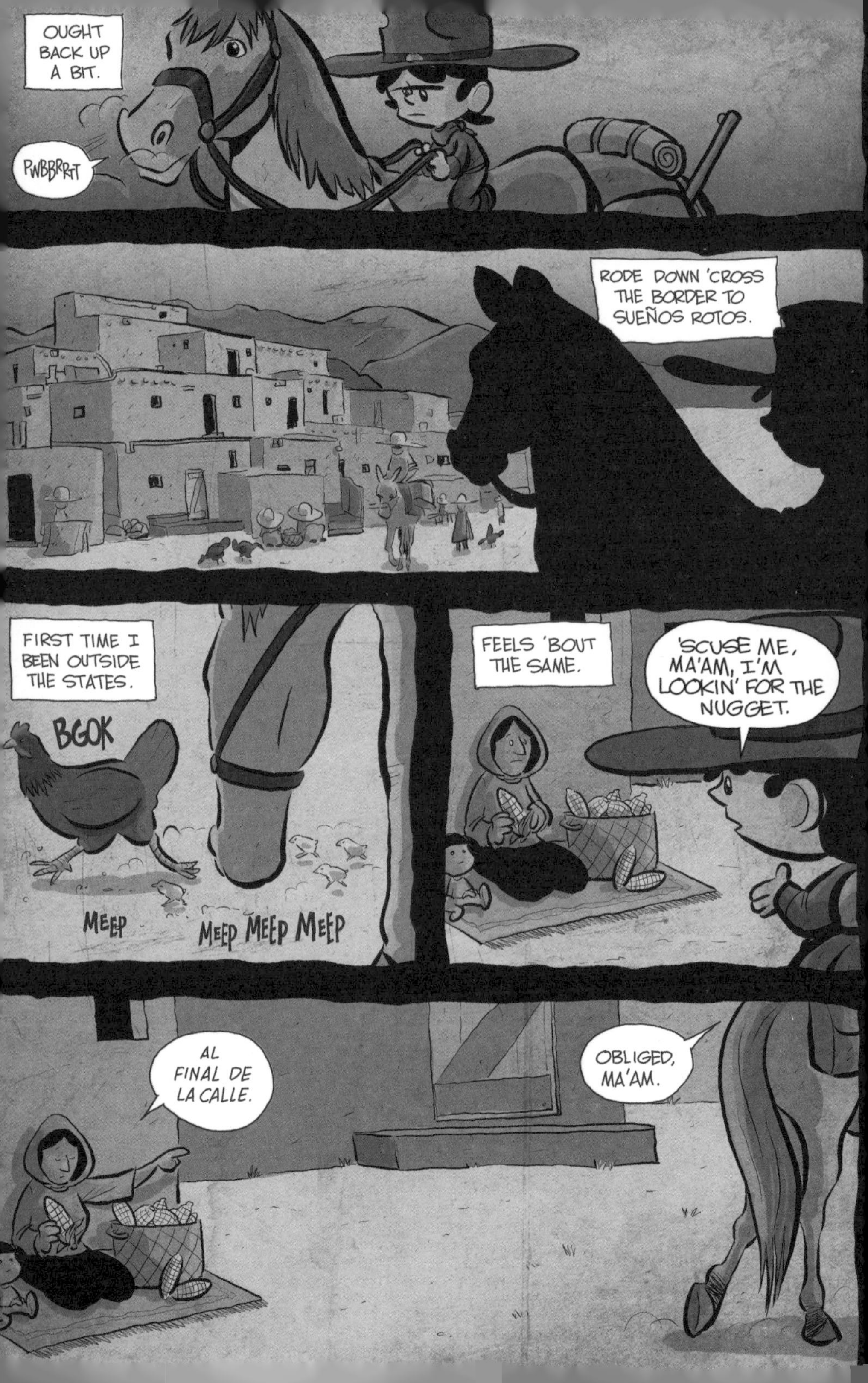

OUGHT BACK UP A BIT.
PWBBRRFT
RODE DOWN 'CROSS THE BORDER TO SUEÑOS ROTOS.
FIRST TIME I BEEN OUTSIDE THE STATES.
BGOK
MEEP
MEEP MEEP MEEP
FEELS 'BOUT THE SAME.
'SCUSE ME, MA'AM, I'M LOOKIN' FOR THE NUGGET.
AL FINAL DE LA CALLE.
OBLIGED, MA'AM.

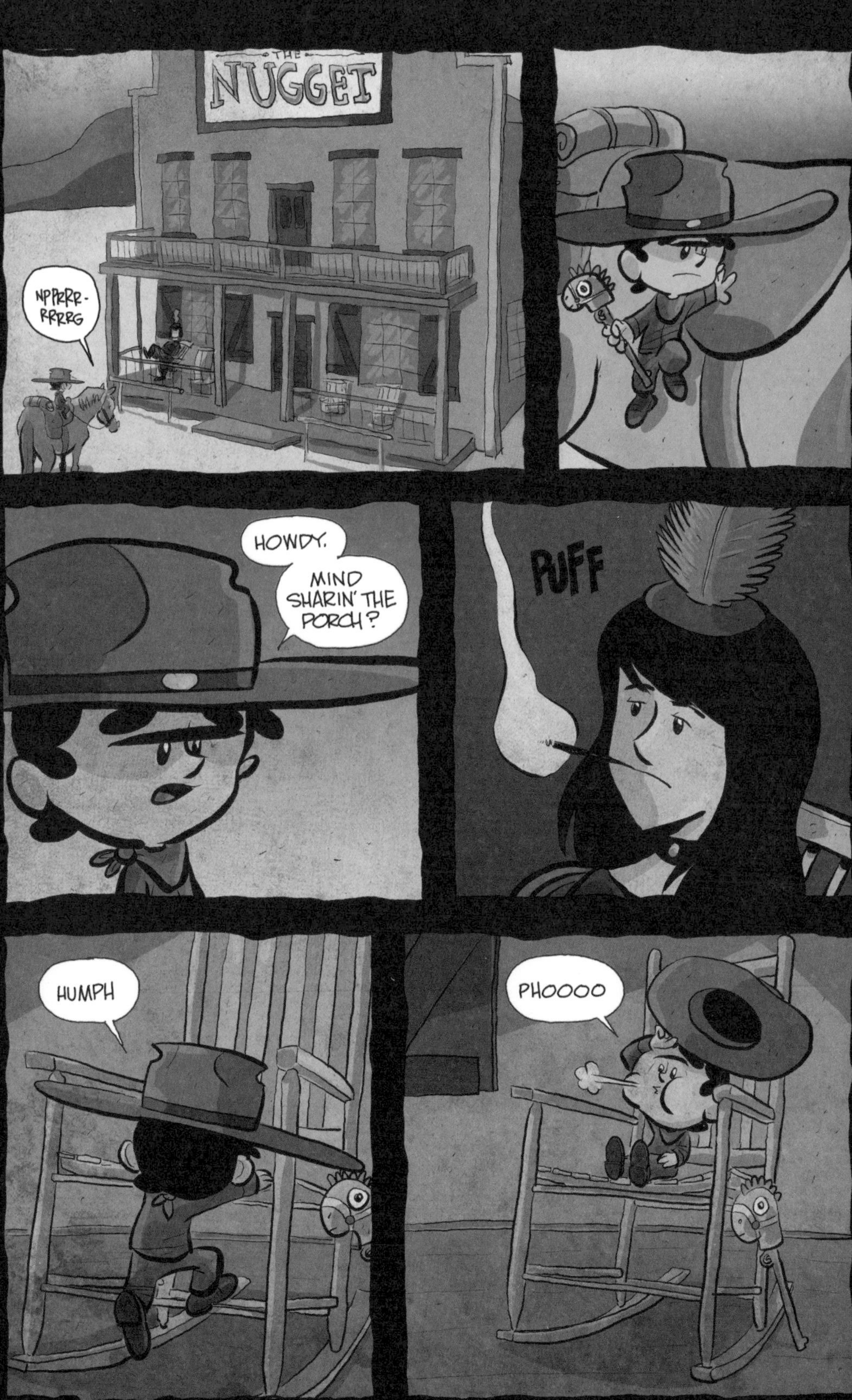
THE NUGGET
NPPRRR-RRRRG
HOWDY.
MIND SHARIN' THE PORCH?
PUFF
HUMPH
PHOOOO

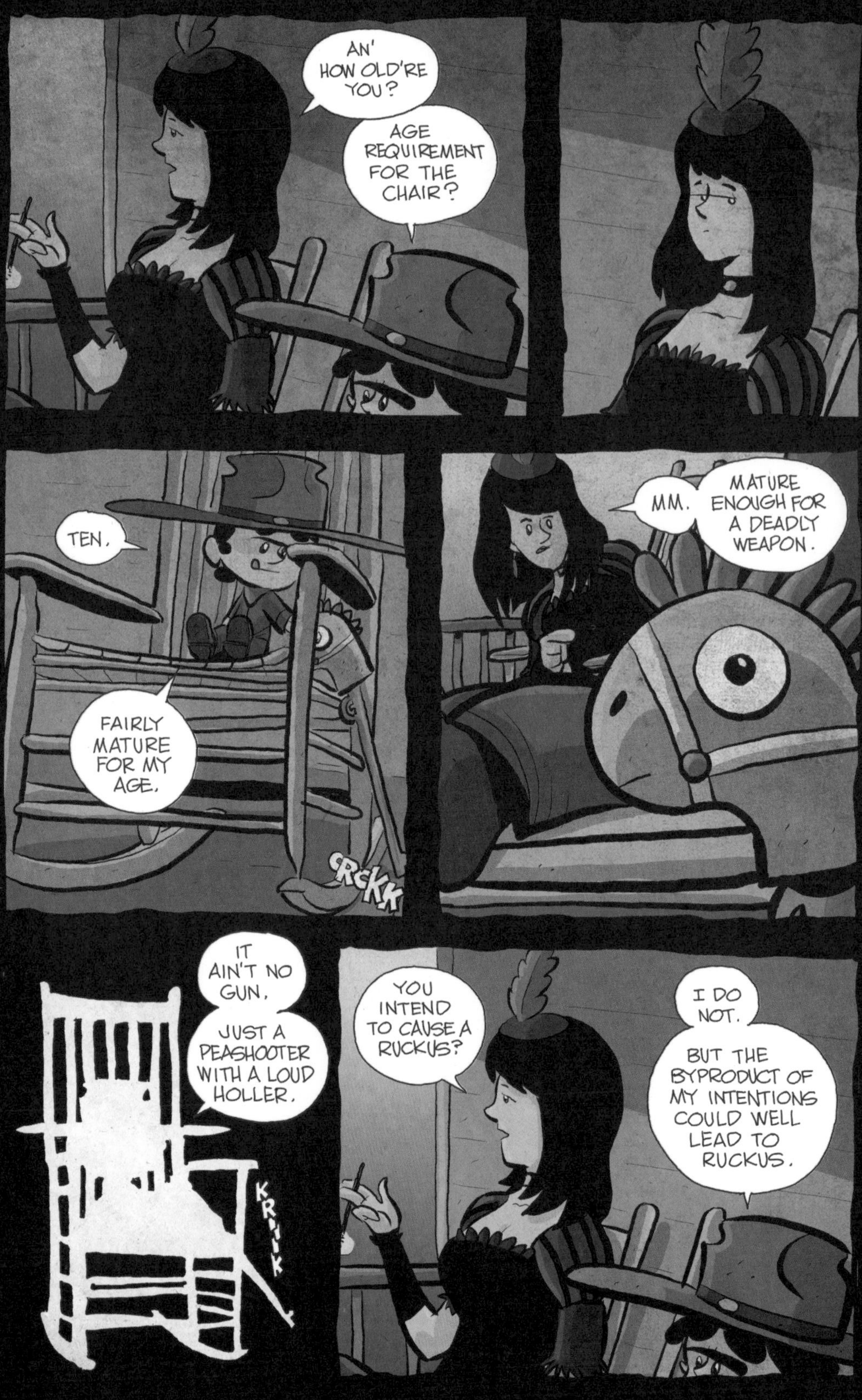
AN' HOW OLD'RE YOU?
AGE REQUIREMENT FOR THE CHAIR?
TEN.
FAIRLY MATURE FOR MY AGE.
CRCKK
MM.
MATURE ENOUGH FOR A DEADLY WEAPON.
IT AIN'T NO GUN.
JUST A PEASHOOTER WITH A LOUD HOLLER.
KRIIK
YOU INTEND TO CAUSE A RUCKUS?
I DO NOT.
BUT THE BYPRODUCT OF MY INTENTIONS COULD WELL LEAD TO RUCKUS.

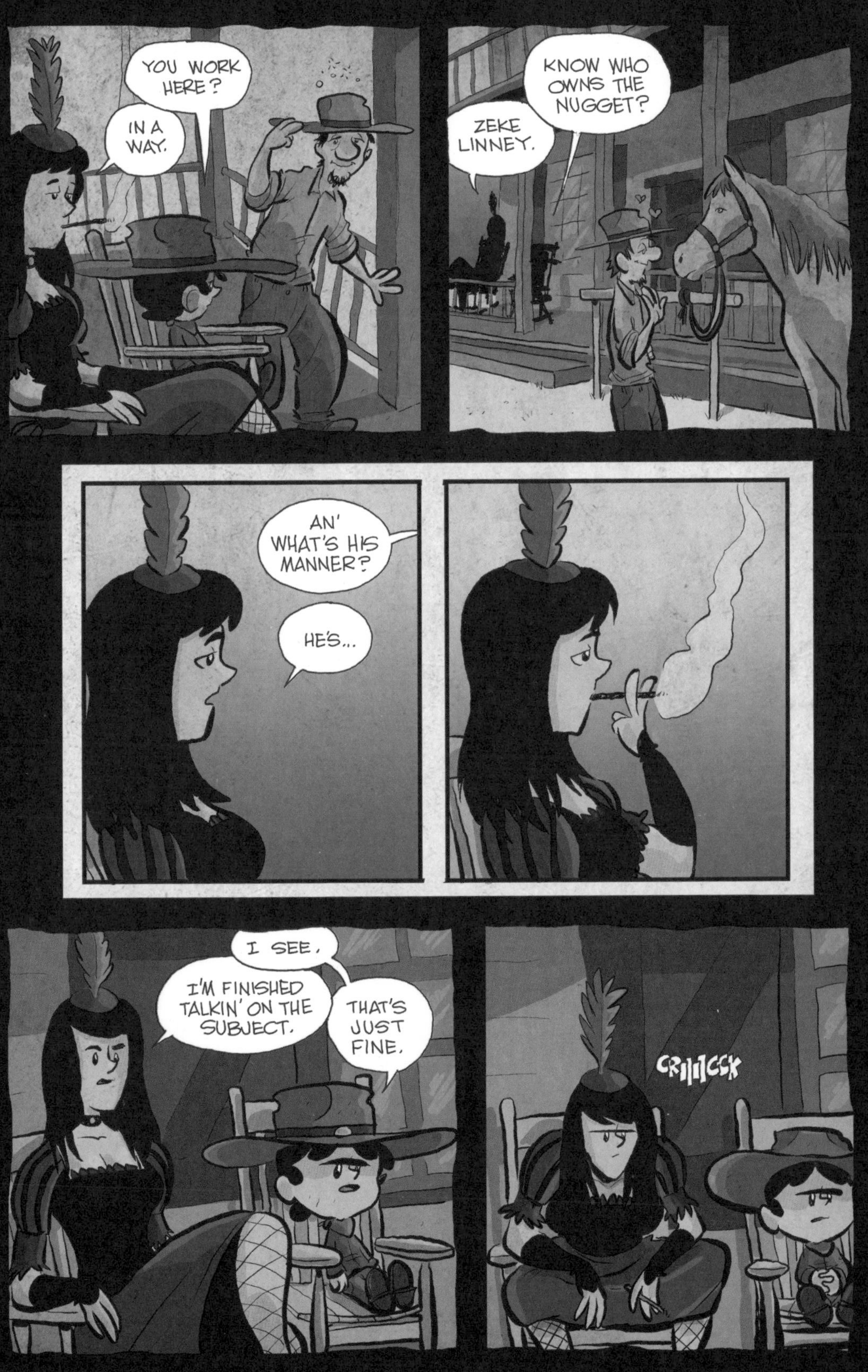
YOU WORK HERE?
IN A WAY.
KNOW WHO OWNS THE NUGGET?
ZEKE LINNEY.
AN' WHAT'S HIS MANNER?
HE'S...
I SEE.
I'M FINISHED TALKIN' ON THE SUBJECT.
THAT'S JUST FINE.
CRIIICCK

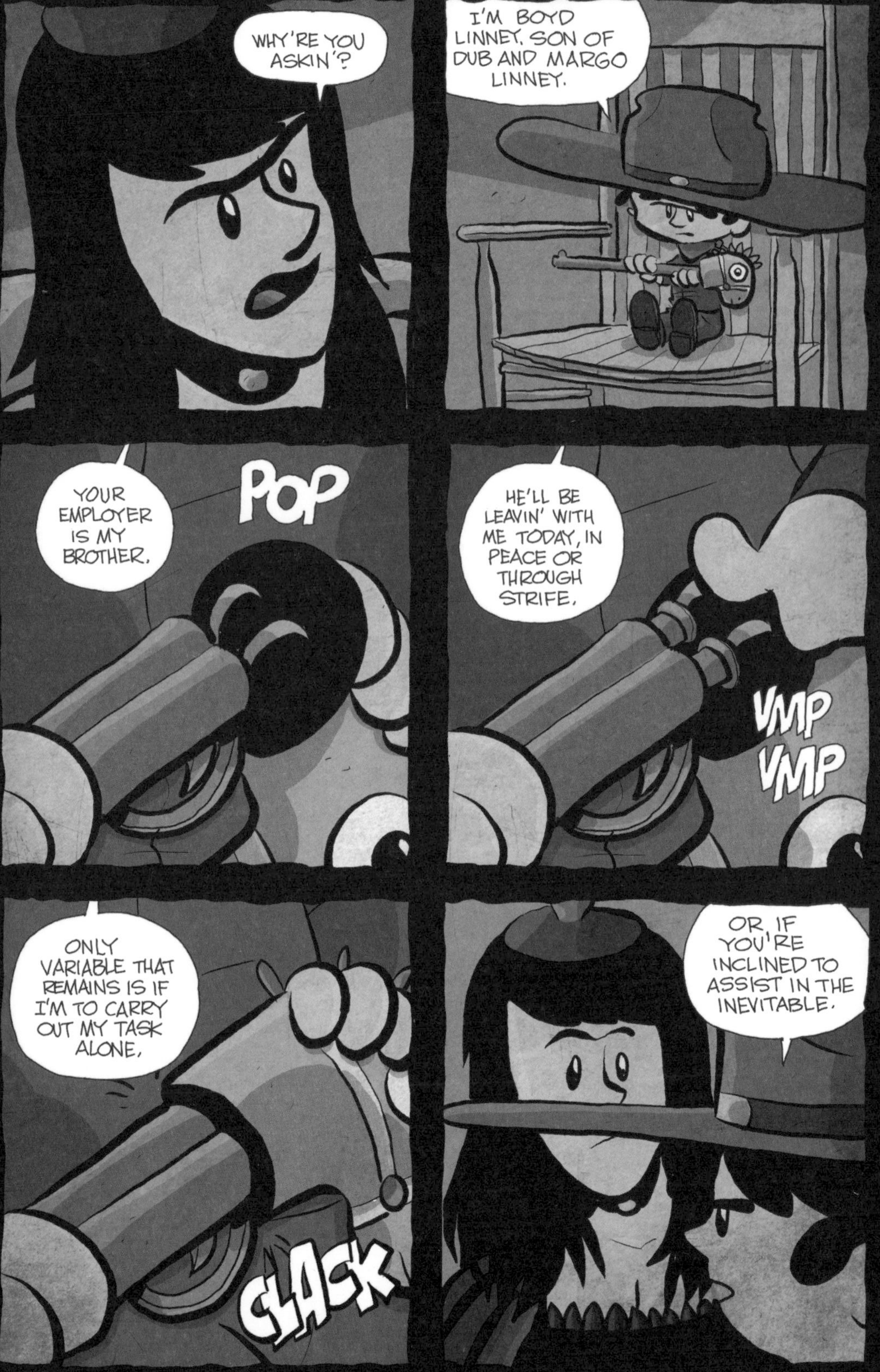
WHY'RE YOU ASKIN'?
I'M BOYD LINNEY. SON OF DUB AND MARGO LINNEY.
YOUR EMPLOYER IS MY BROTHER.
POP
HE'LL BE LEAVIN' WITH ME TODAY, IN PEACE OR THROUGH STRIFE.
VMP VMP
ONLY VARIABLE THAT REMAINS IS IF I'M TO CARRY OUT MY TASK ALONE,
CLACK
OR, IF YOU'RE INCLINED TO ASSIST IN THE INEVITABLE.

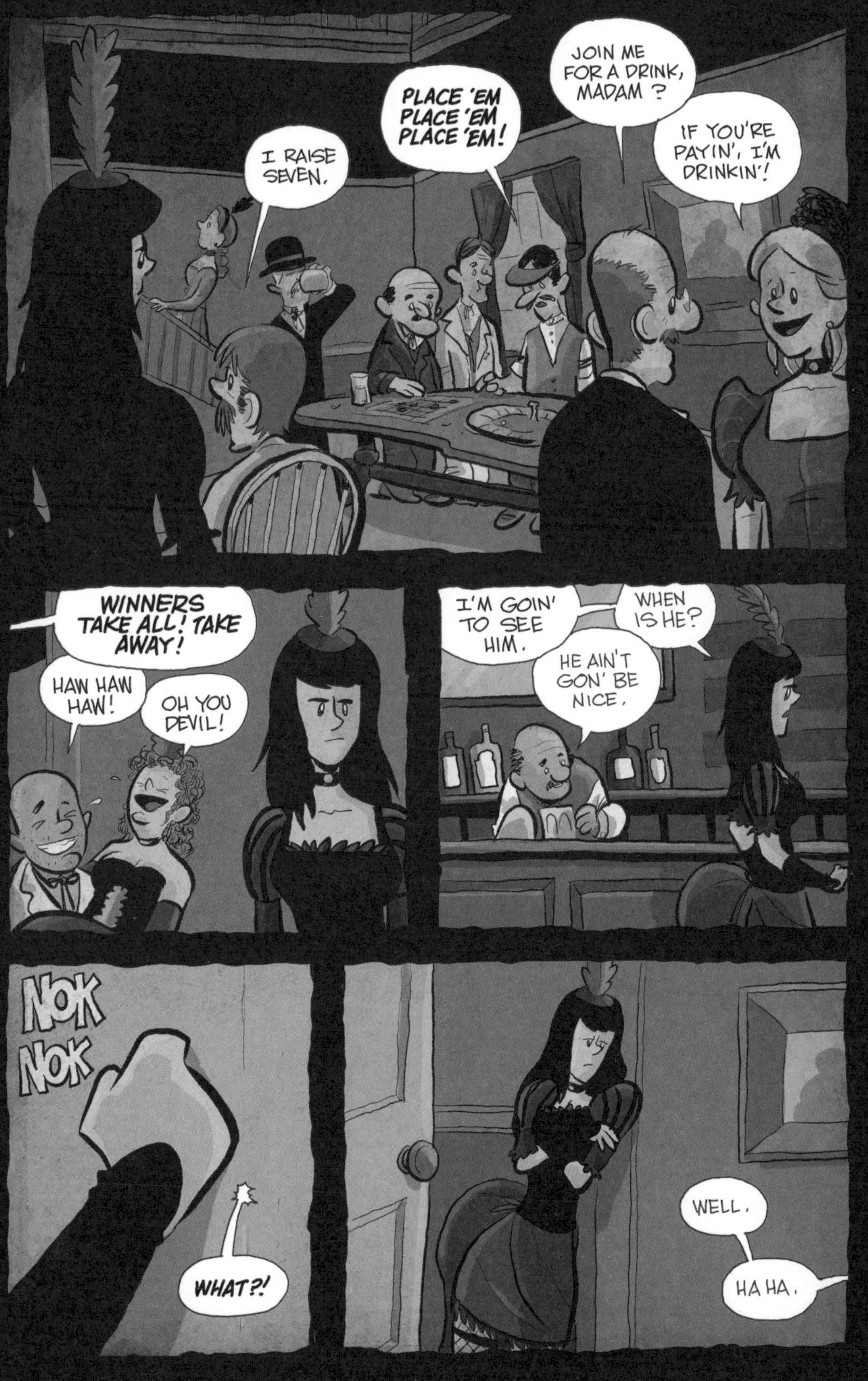
I RAISE SEVEN.
PLACE 'EM PLACE 'EM PLACE 'EM!
JOIN ME FOR A DRINK, MADAM ?
IF YOU'RE PAYIN', I'M DRINKIN'!
WINNERS TAKE ALL! TAKE AWAY!
HAW HAW HAW!
OH YOU DEVIL!
I'M GOIN' TO SEE HIM.
WHEN IS HE?
HE AIN'T GON' BE NICE.
NOK NOK
WHAT?!
WELL.
HA HA.

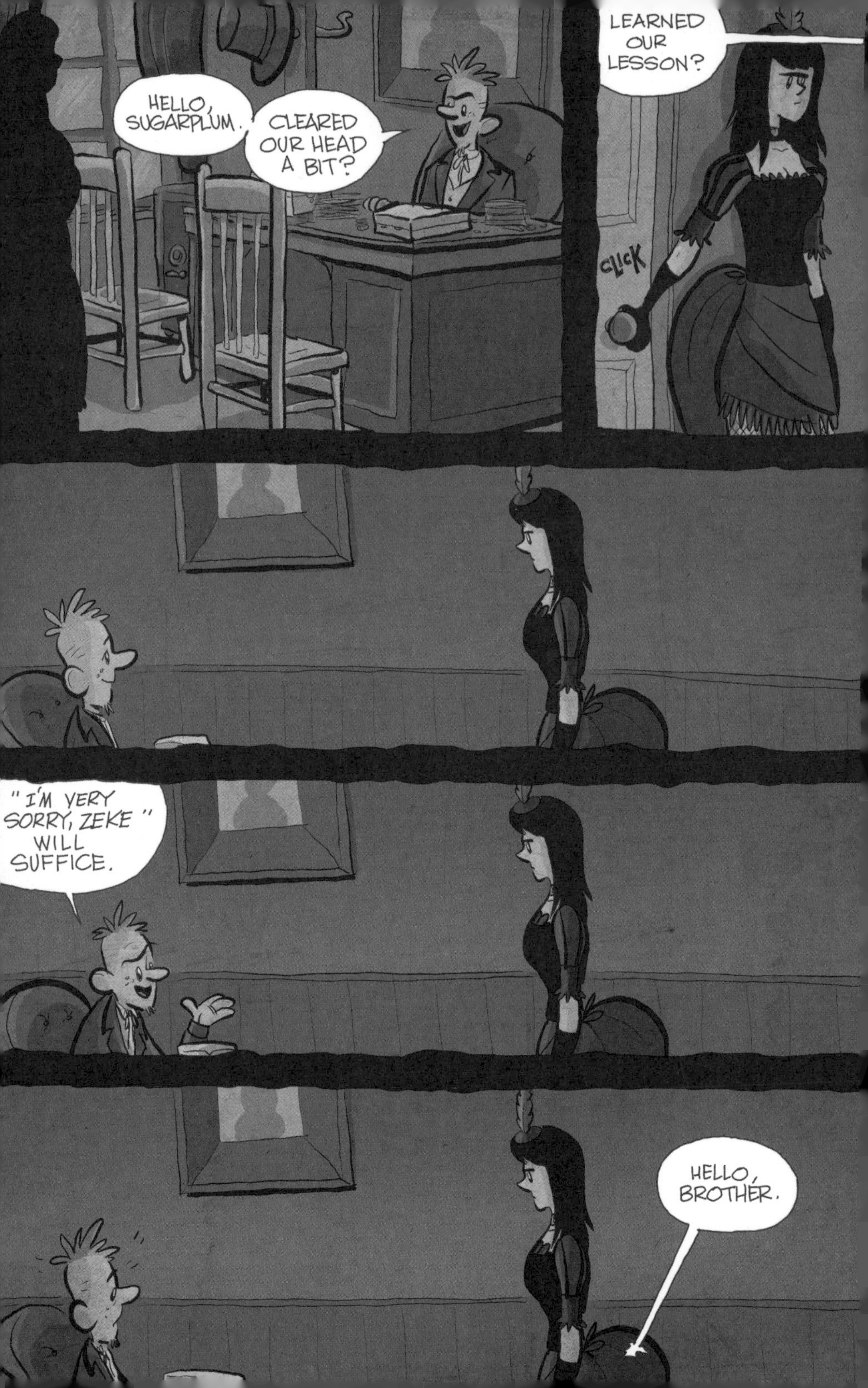
HELLO, SUGARPLUM.
CLEARED OUR HEAD A BIT?
LEARNED OUR LESSON?
CLICK
"I'M VERY SORRY, ZEKE" WILL SUFFICE.
HELLO, BROTHER.

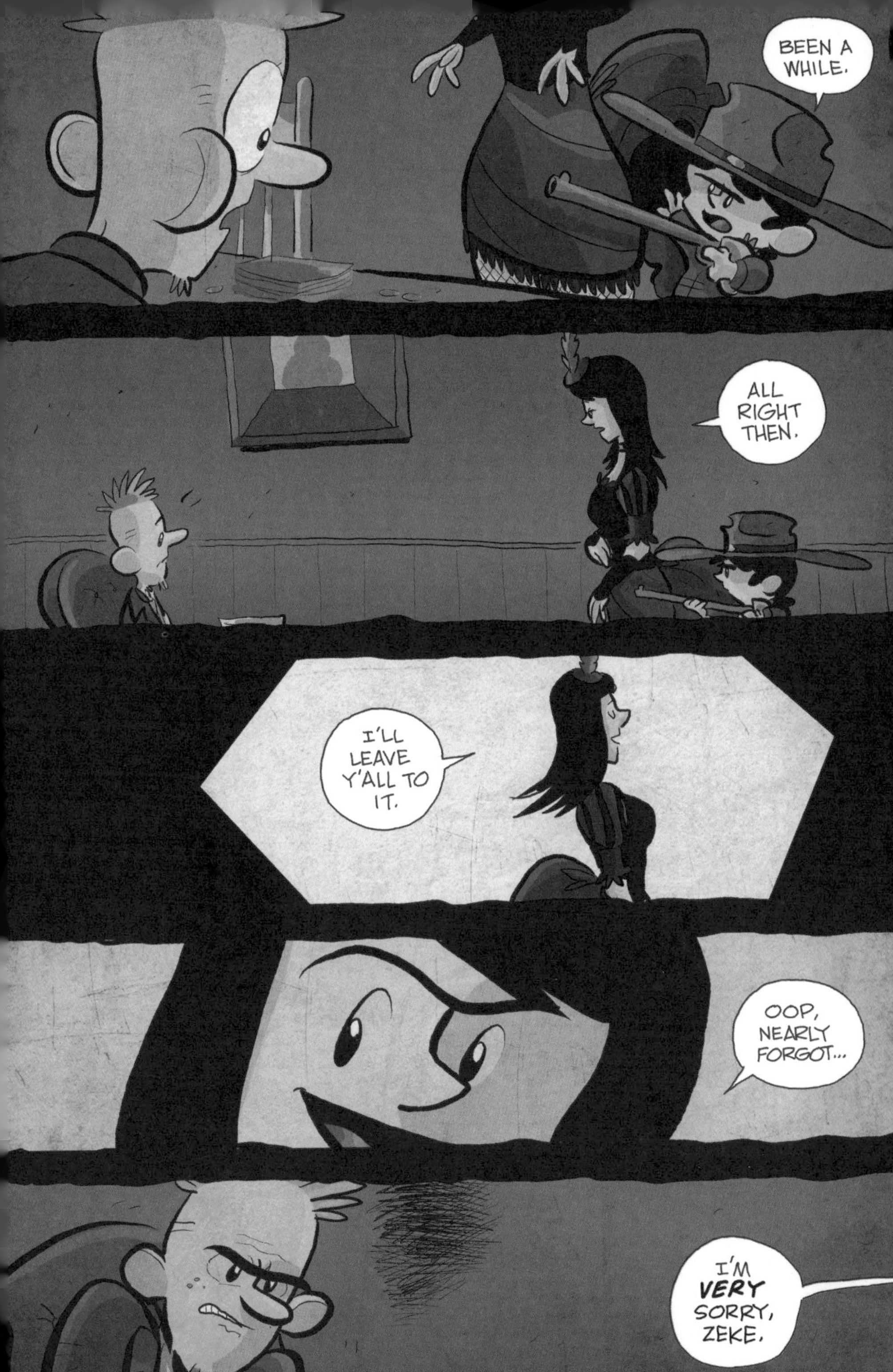
BEEN A WHILE.
ALL RIGHT THEN.
I'LL LEAVE Y'ALL TO IT.
OOP, NEARLY FORGOT...
I'M **VERY** SORRY, ZEKE.

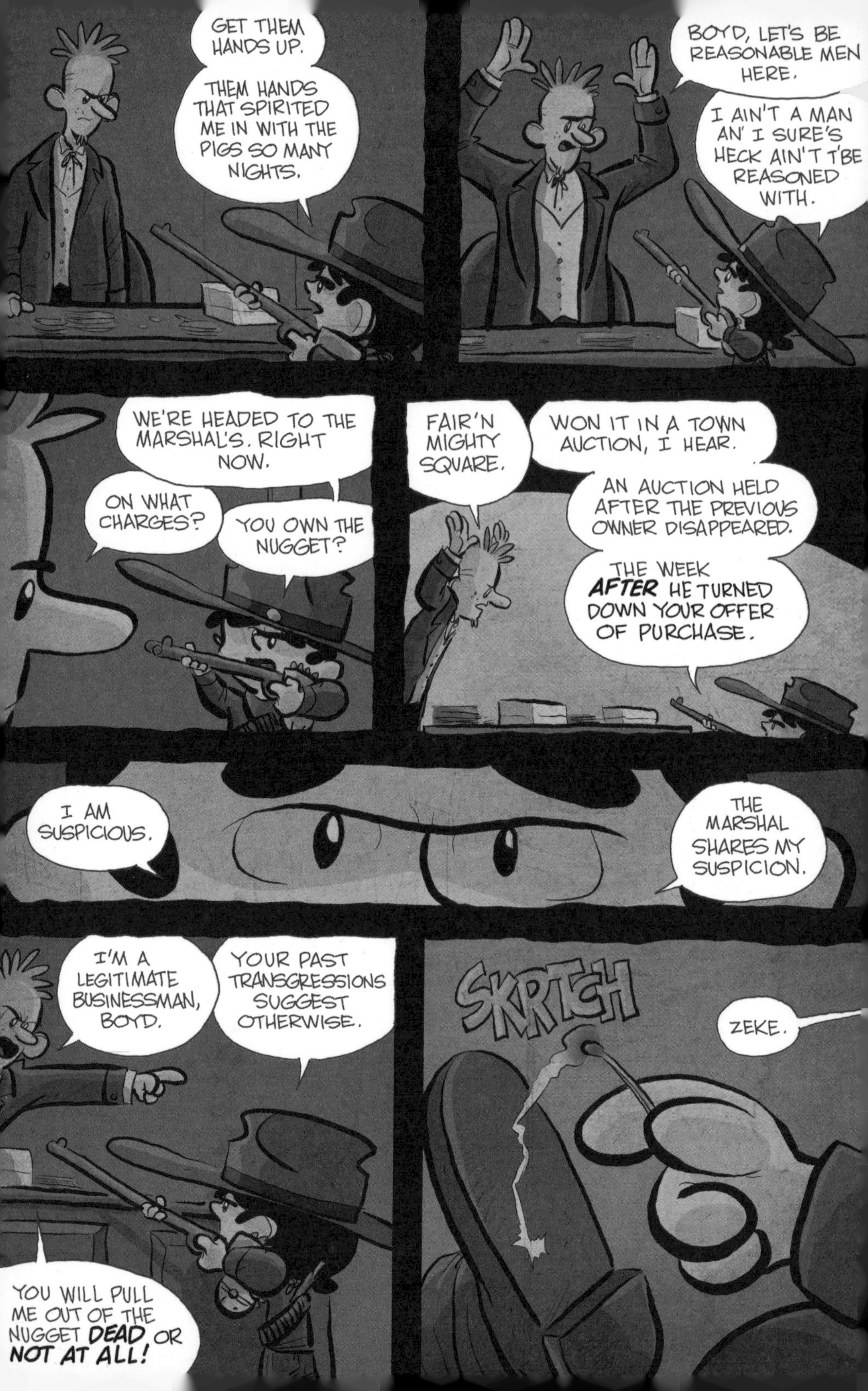
GET THEM HANDS UP.
THEM HANDS THAT SPIRITED ME IN WITH THE PIGS SO MANY NIGHTS.
BOYD, LET'S BE REASONABLE MEN HERE.
I AIN'T A MAN AN' I SURE'S HECK AIN'T T'BE REASONED WITH.
WE'RE HEADED TO THE MARSHAL'S. RIGHT NOW.
ON WHAT CHARGES?
YOU OWN THE NUGGET?
FAIR'N MIGHTY SQUARE.
WON IT IN A TOWN AUCTION, I HEAR.
AN AUCTION HELD AFTER THE PREVIOUS OWNER DISAPPEARED.
THE WEEK **AFTER** HE TURNED DOWN YOUR OFFER OF PURCHASE.
I AM SUSPICIOUS.
THE MARSHAL SHARES MY SUSPICION.
I'M A LEGITIMATE BUSINESSMAN, BOYD.
YOUR PAST TRANSGRESSIONS SUGGEST OTHERWISE.
YOU WILL PULL ME OUT OF THE NUGGET **DEAD** OR **NOT AT ALL!**
SKRTCH
ZEKE.

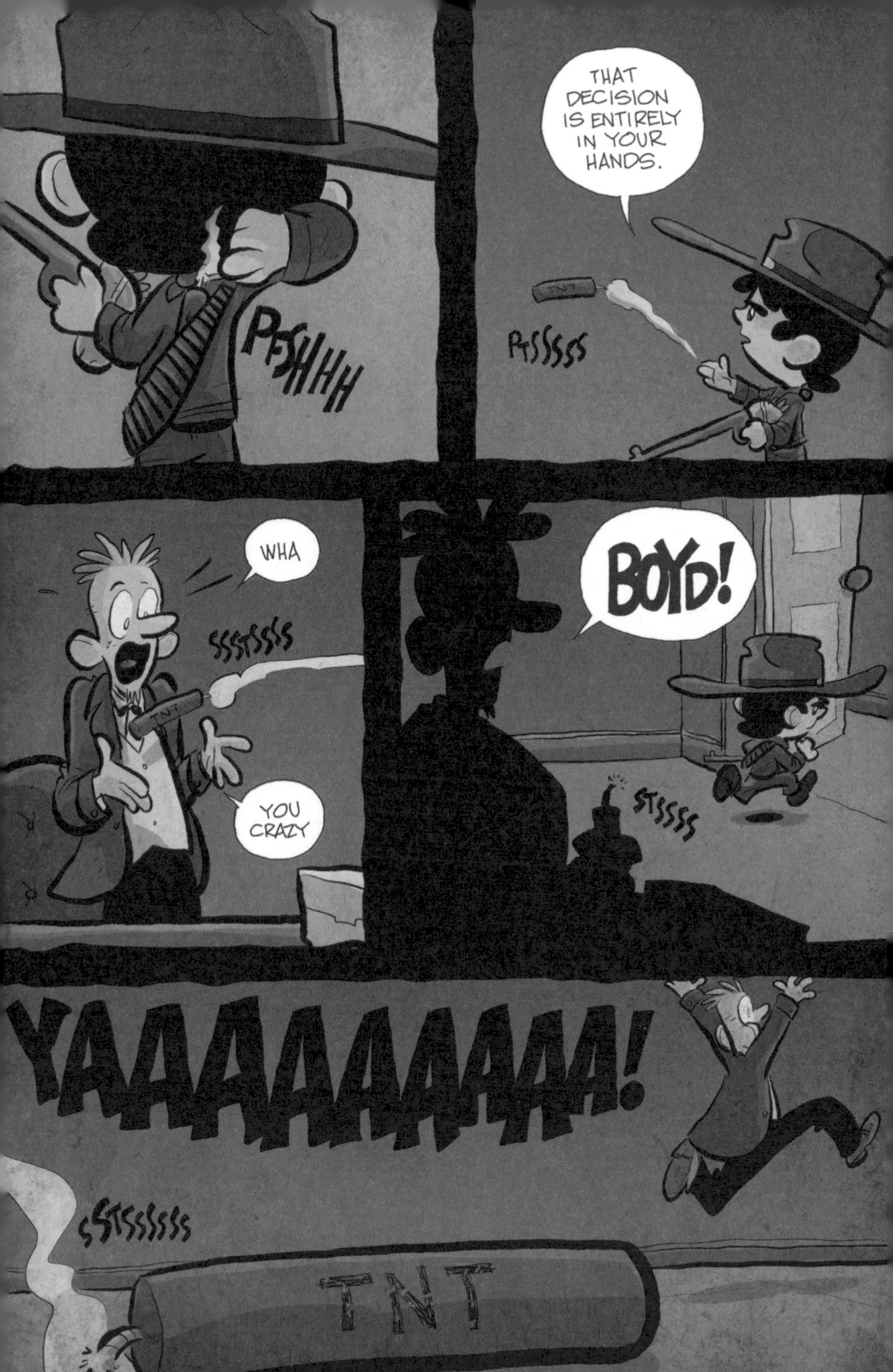
PFSHHH
THAT DECISION IS ENTIRELY IN YOUR HANDS.
PTSSSSS
WHA
SSSTSSSS
YOU CRAZY
BOYD!
STSSSS
YAAAAAAAAA!
SSTSSSSSS
TNT

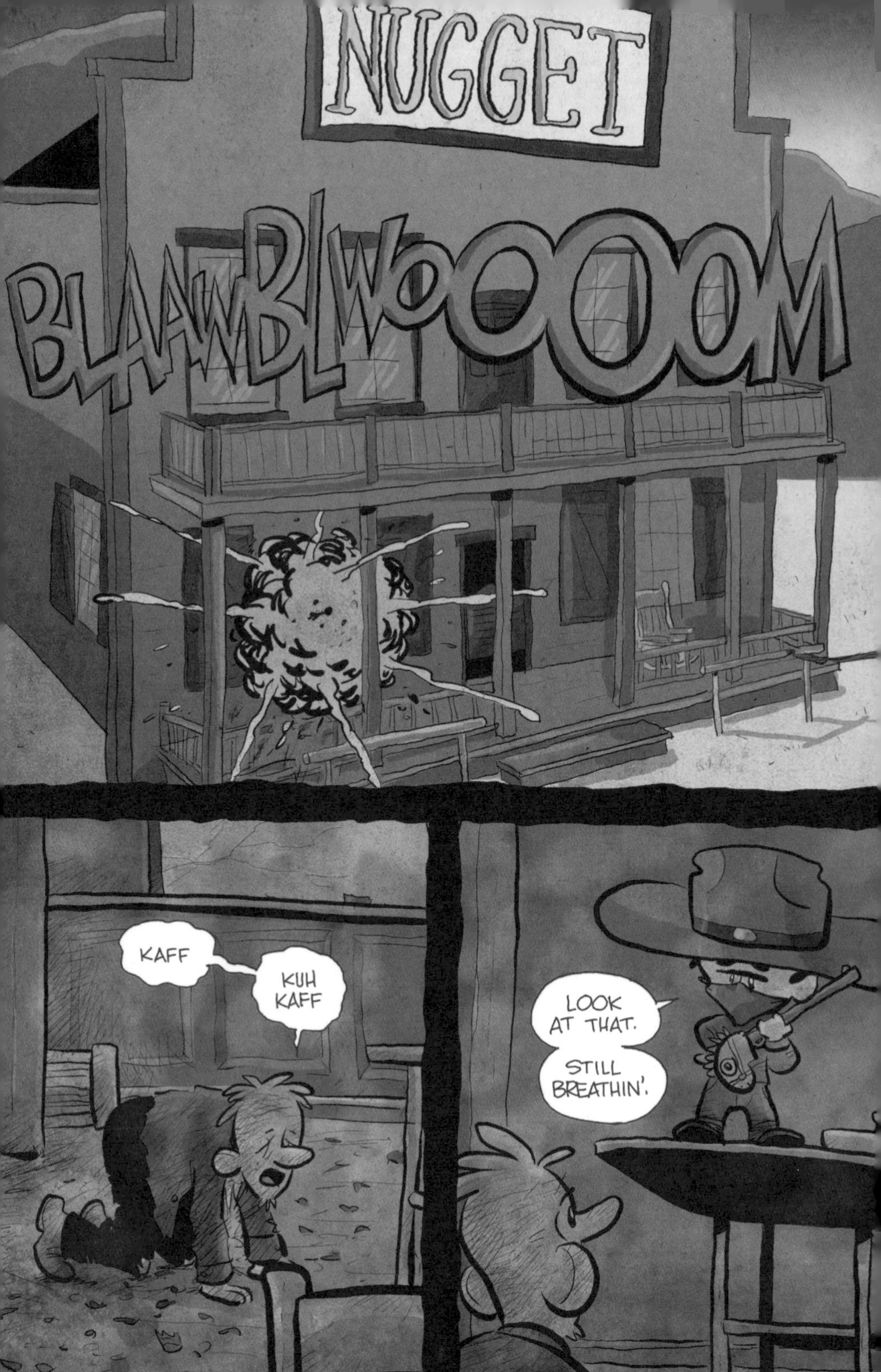
NUGGET
BLAAWBLWOOOOOM
KAFF
KUH KAFF
LOOK AT THAT.
STILL BREATHIN'.

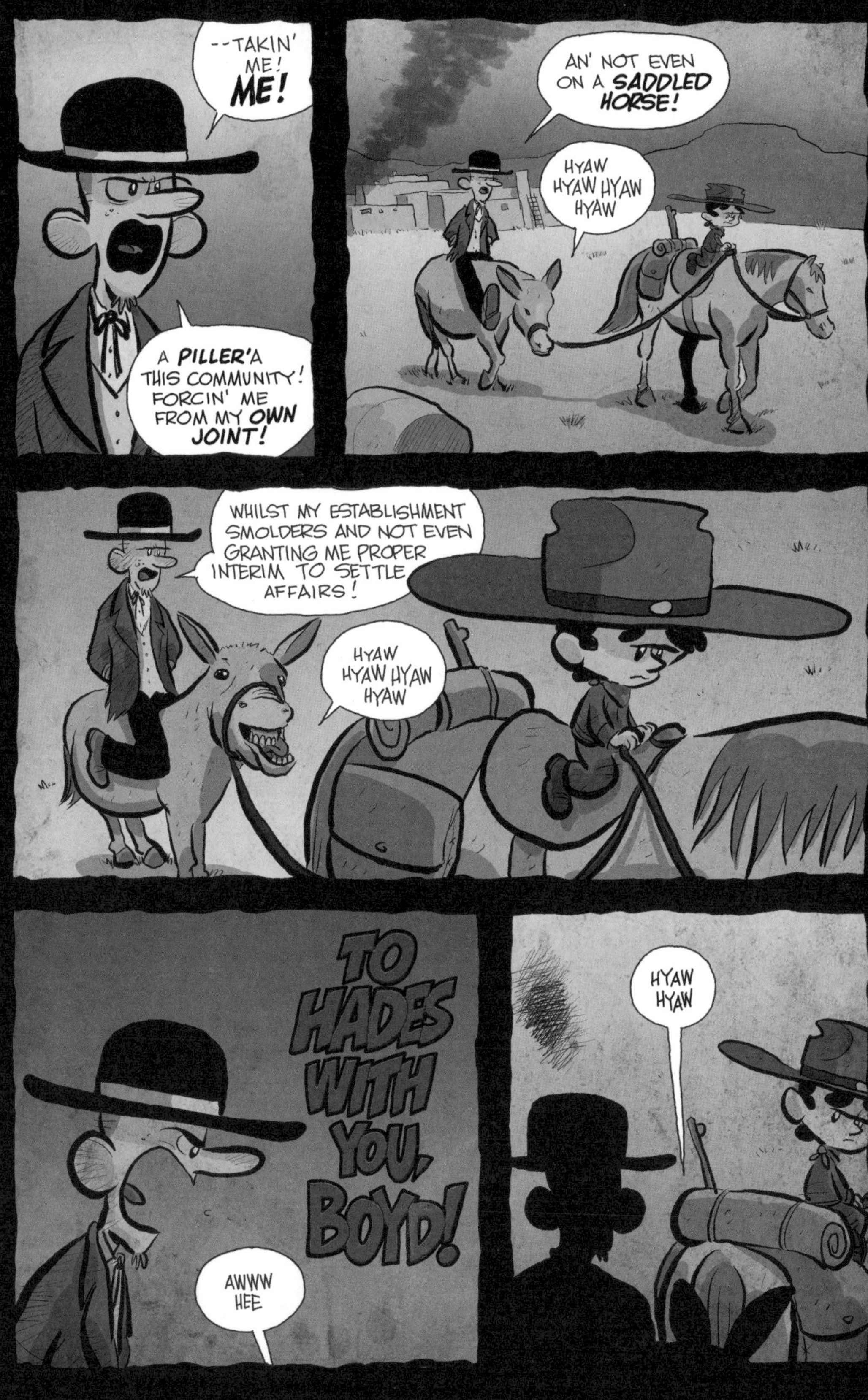
--TAKIN' ME! **ME!**
A **PILLER**'A THIS COMMUNITY! FORCIN' ME FROM MY **OWN** **JOINT!**
AN' NOT EVEN ON A **SADDLED HORSE!**
HYAW HYAW HYAW HYAW
WHILST MY ESTABLISHMENT SMOLDERS AND NOT EVEN GRANTING ME PROPER INTERIM TO SETTLE AFFAIRS!
HYAW HYAW HYAW HYAW
TO HADES WITH YOU, BOYD!
AWWW HEE
HYAW HYAW

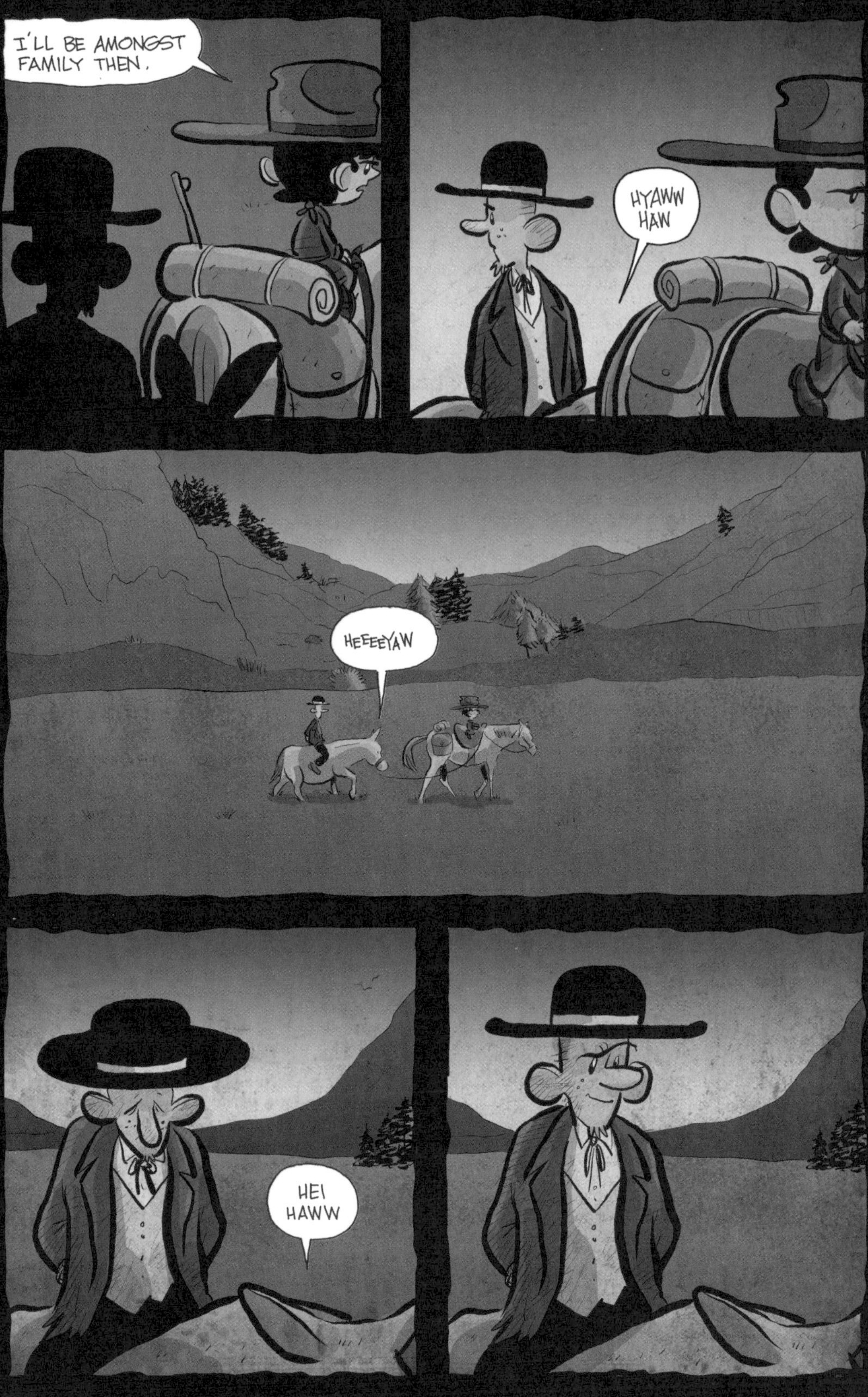

I'LL BE AMONGST FAMILY THEN.
HYAWW HAW
HEEEEYAW
HEI HAWW

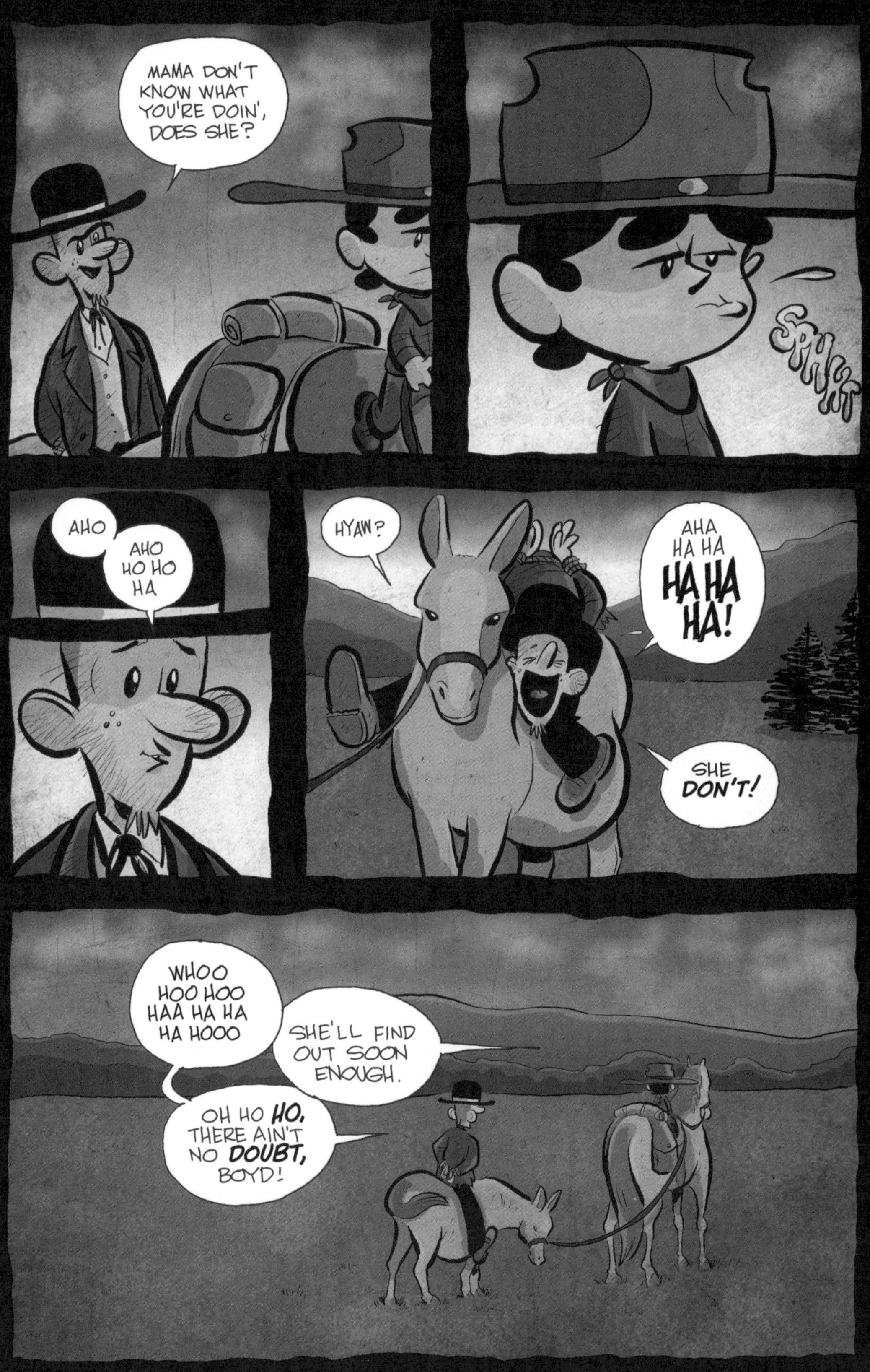
MAMA DON'T KNOW WHAT YOU'RE DOIN', DOES SHE?
SPHHT
AHO
AHO HO HO HA
HYAW?
AHA HA HA HA HA HA!
SHE DON'T!
WHOO HOO HOO HAA HA HA HA HOOO
SHE'LL FIND OUT SOON ENOUGH.
OH HO HO, THERE AIN'T NO DOUBT, BOYD!

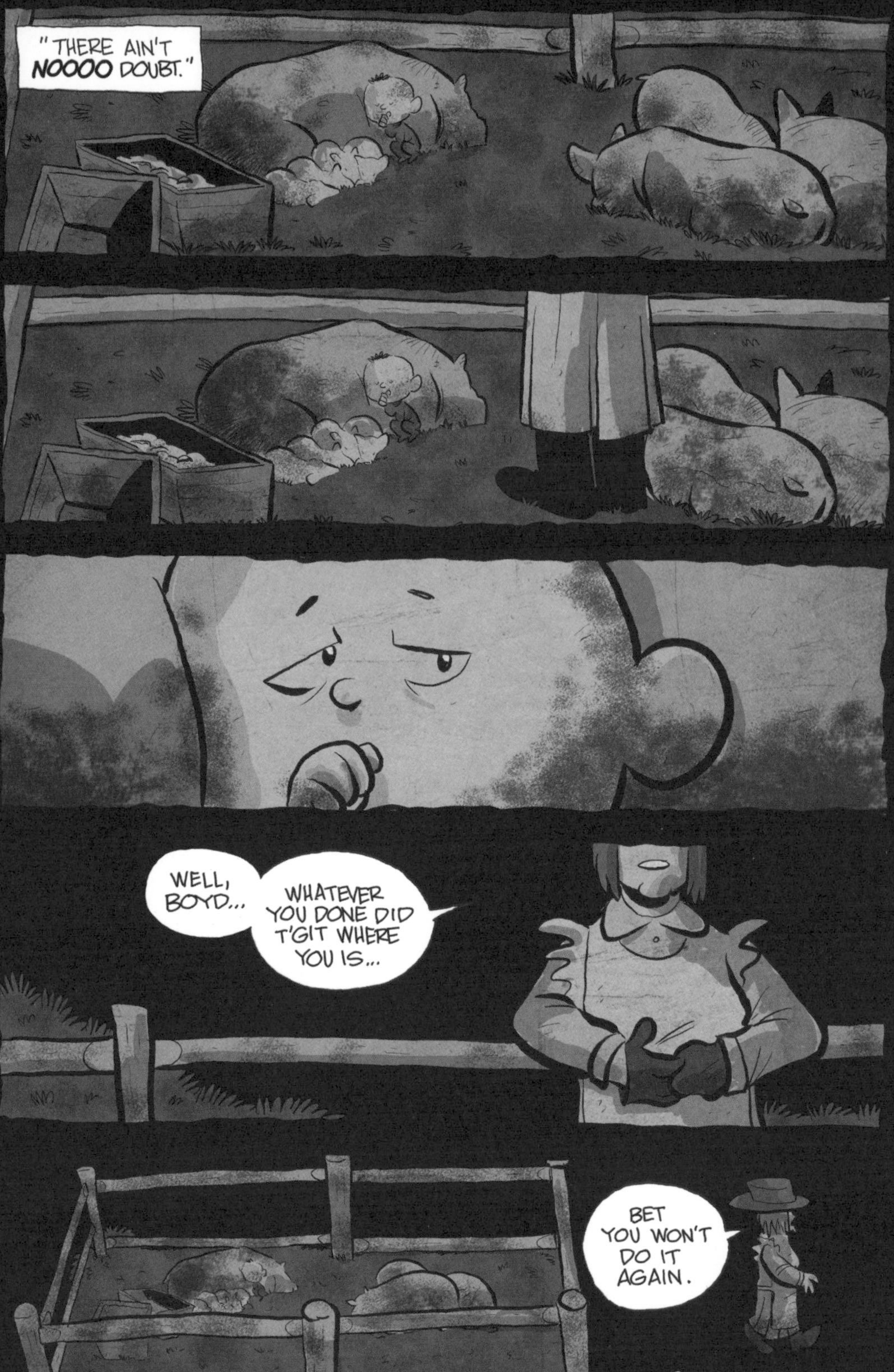
"THERE AIN'T **NOOOO** DOUBT."
WELL, BOYD...
WHATEVER YOU DONE DID T'GIT WHERE YOU IS...
BET YOU WON'T DO IT AGAIN.
CONTINUED.

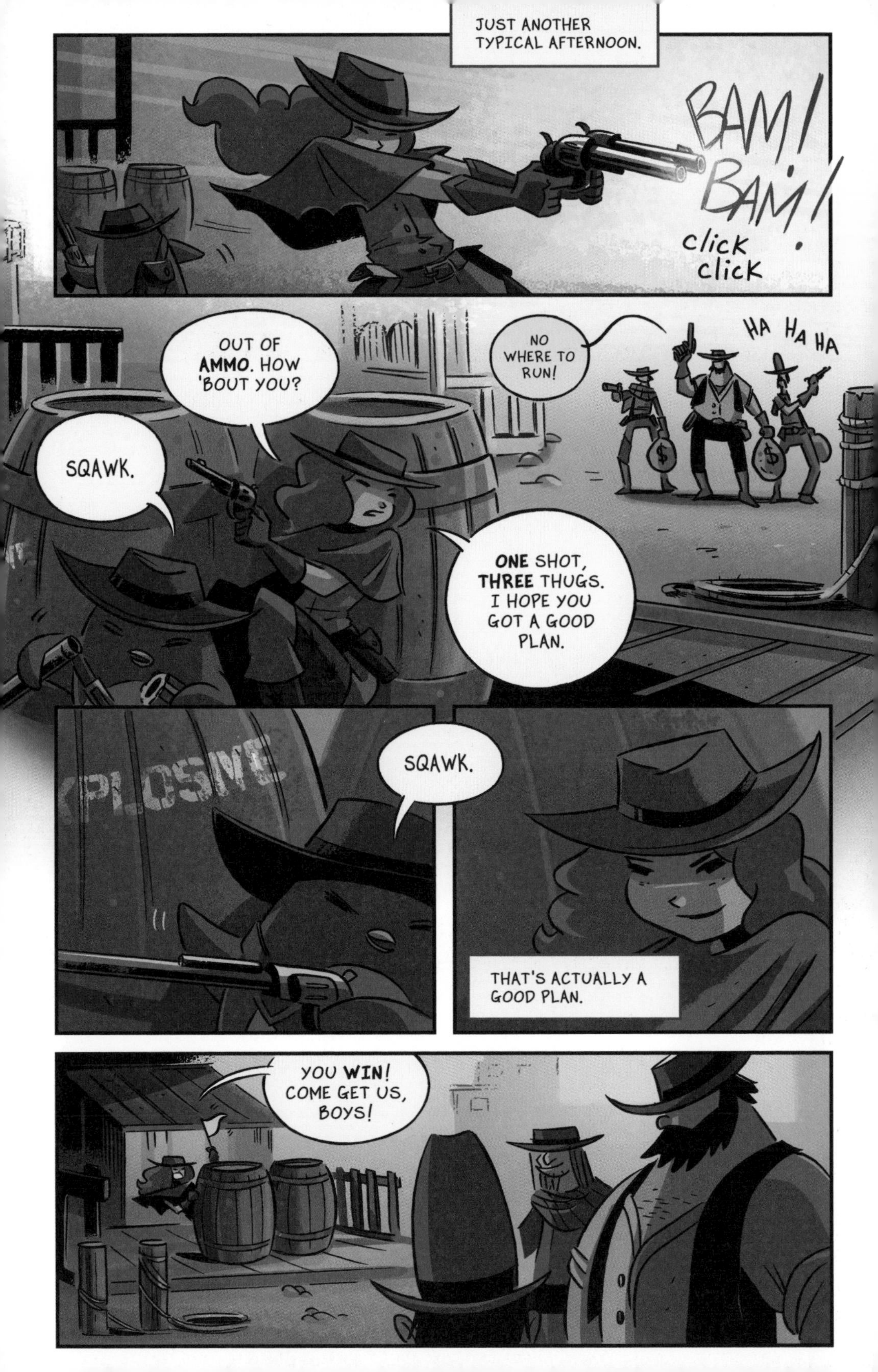
JUST ANOTHER TYPICAL AFTERNOON.
BAM! BAM!
click click
OUT OF AMMO. HOW 'BOUT YOU?
NO WHERE TO RUN!
HA HA HA
SQAWK.
ONE SHOT, THREE THUGS. I HOPE YOU GOT A GOOD PLAN.
XPLOSIVE
SQAWK.
THAT'S ACTUALLY A GOOD PLAN.
YOU WIN! COME GET US, BOYS!

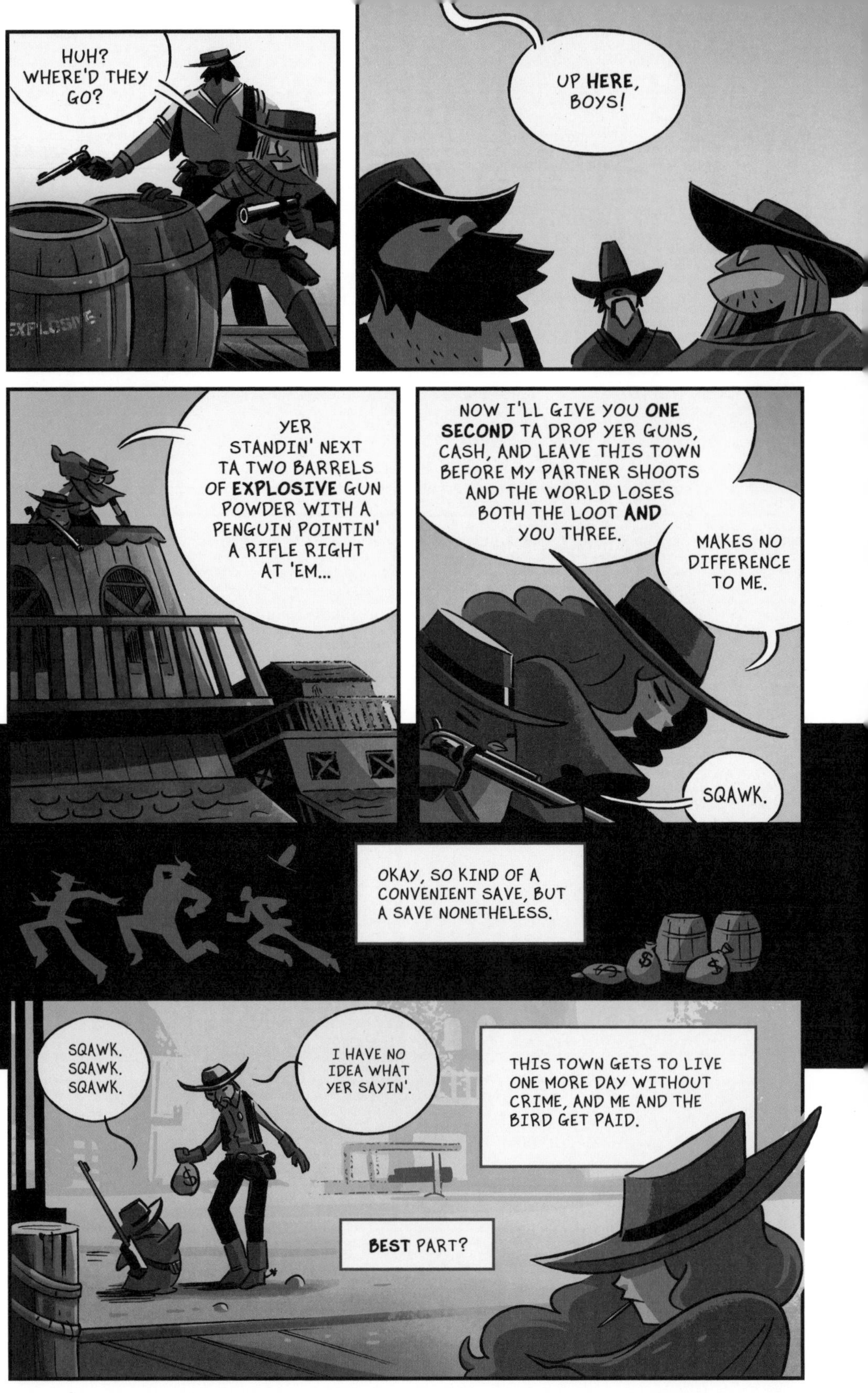
HUH? WHERE'D THEY GO?
UP **HERE**, BOYS!
YER STANDIN' NEXT TA TWO BARRELS OF **EXPLOSIVE** GUN POWDER WITH A PENGUIN POINTIN' A RIFLE RIGHT AT 'EM...
EXPLOSIVE
NOW I'LL GIVE YOU **ONE SECOND** TA DROP YER GUNS, CASH, AND LEAVE THIS TOWN BEFORE MY PARTNER SHOOTS AND THE WORLD LOSES BOTH THE LOOT **AND** YOU THREE.
MAKES NO DIFFERENCE TO ME.
SQAWK.
OKAY, SO KIND OF A CONVENIENT SAVE, BUT A SAVE NONETHELESS.
SQAWK. SQAWK. SQAWK.
I HAVE NO IDEA WHAT YER SAYIN'.
THIS TOWN GETS TO LIVE ONE MORE DAY WITHOUT CRIME, AND ME AND THE BIRD GET PAID.
BEST PART?

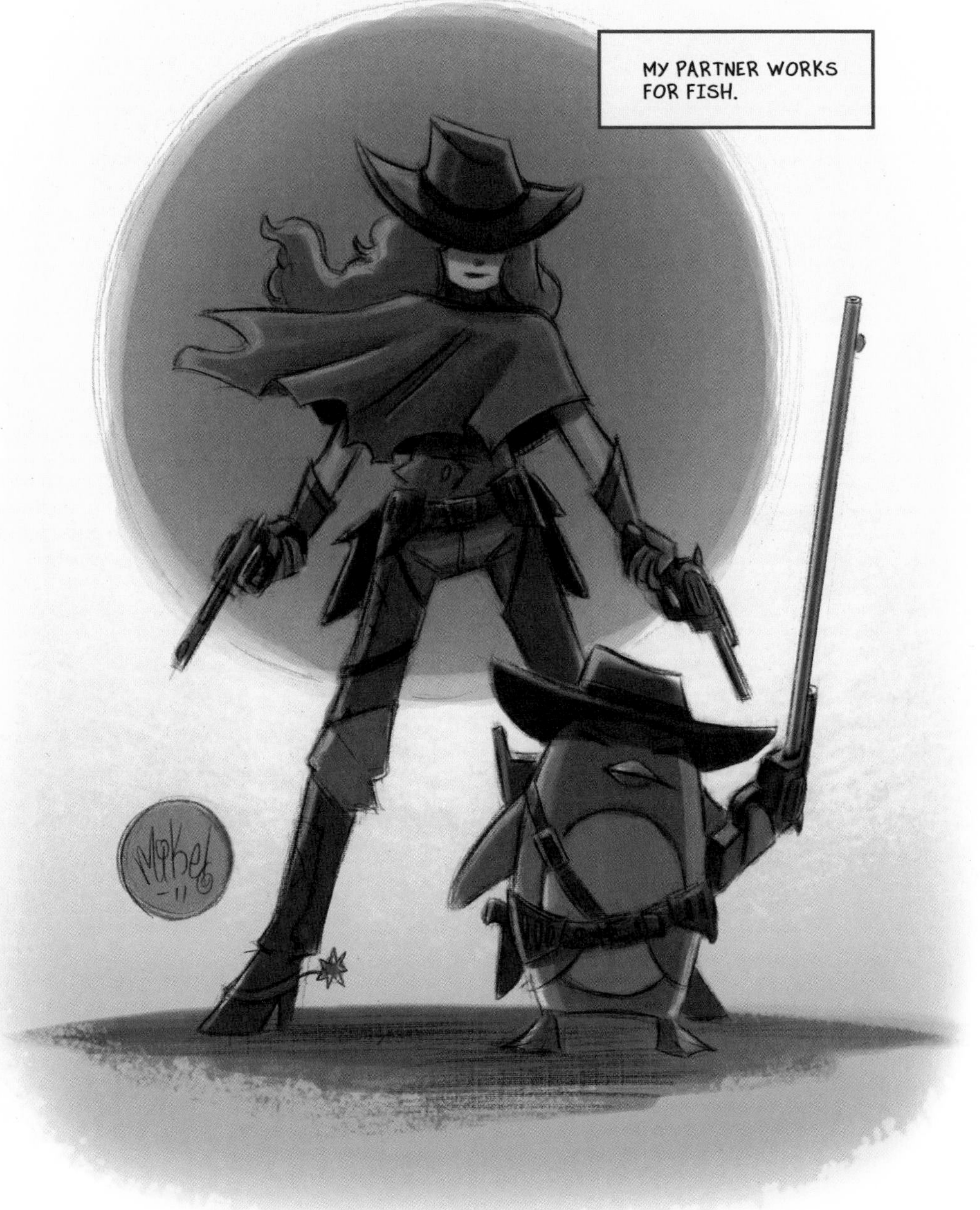
MY PARTNER WORKS
FOR FISH.

A PENGUIN NEVER MISSES

STORY AND ART BY
MIKE MAIHACK

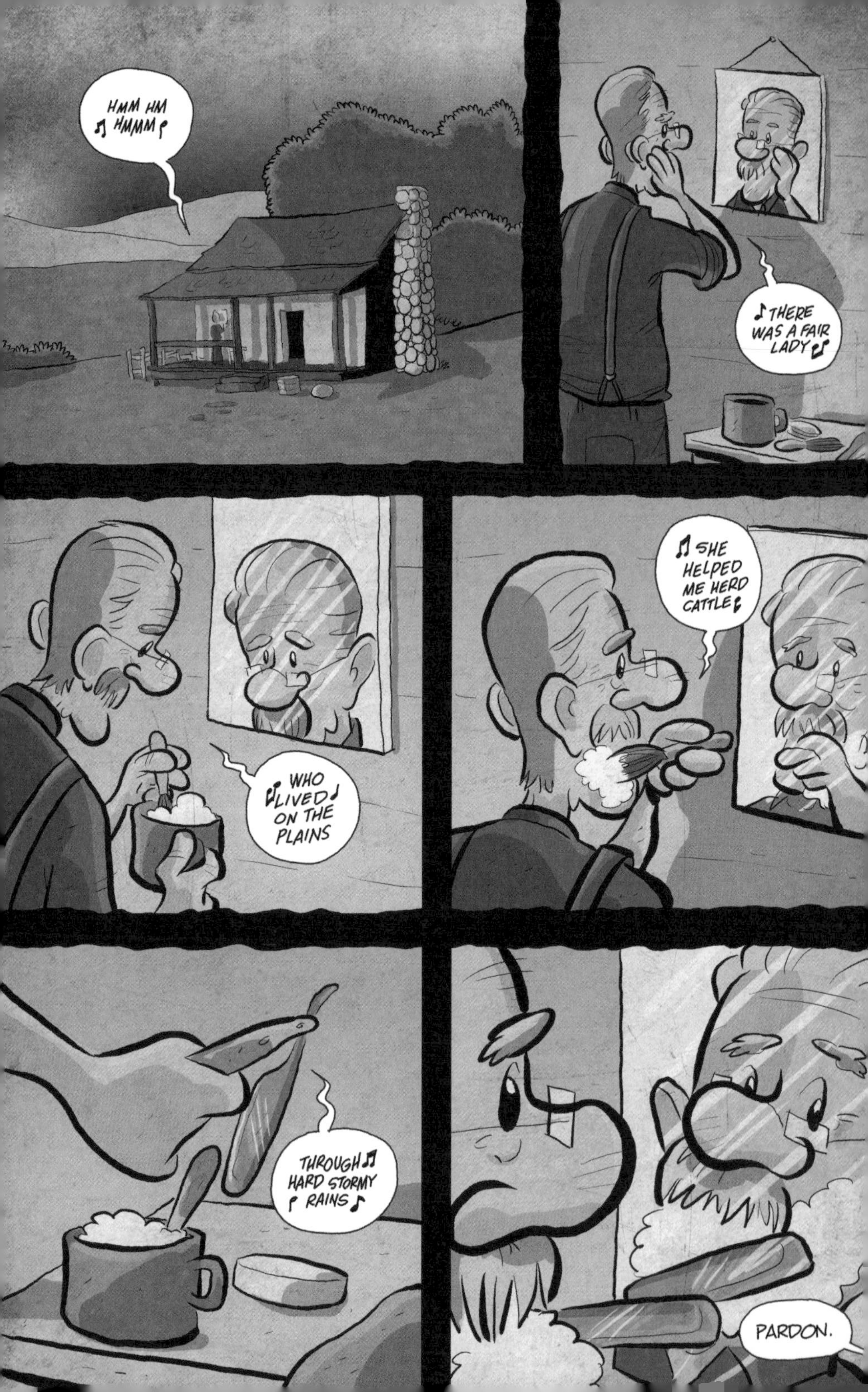
HMM HM ♪ HMMM ♪
♪ THERE WAS A FAIR LADY ♪
♪ WHO LIVED ♪ ON THE PLAINS
♫ SHE HELPED ME HERD CATTLE ♪
THROUGH ♫ HARD STORMY ♪ RAINS ♪
PARDON.

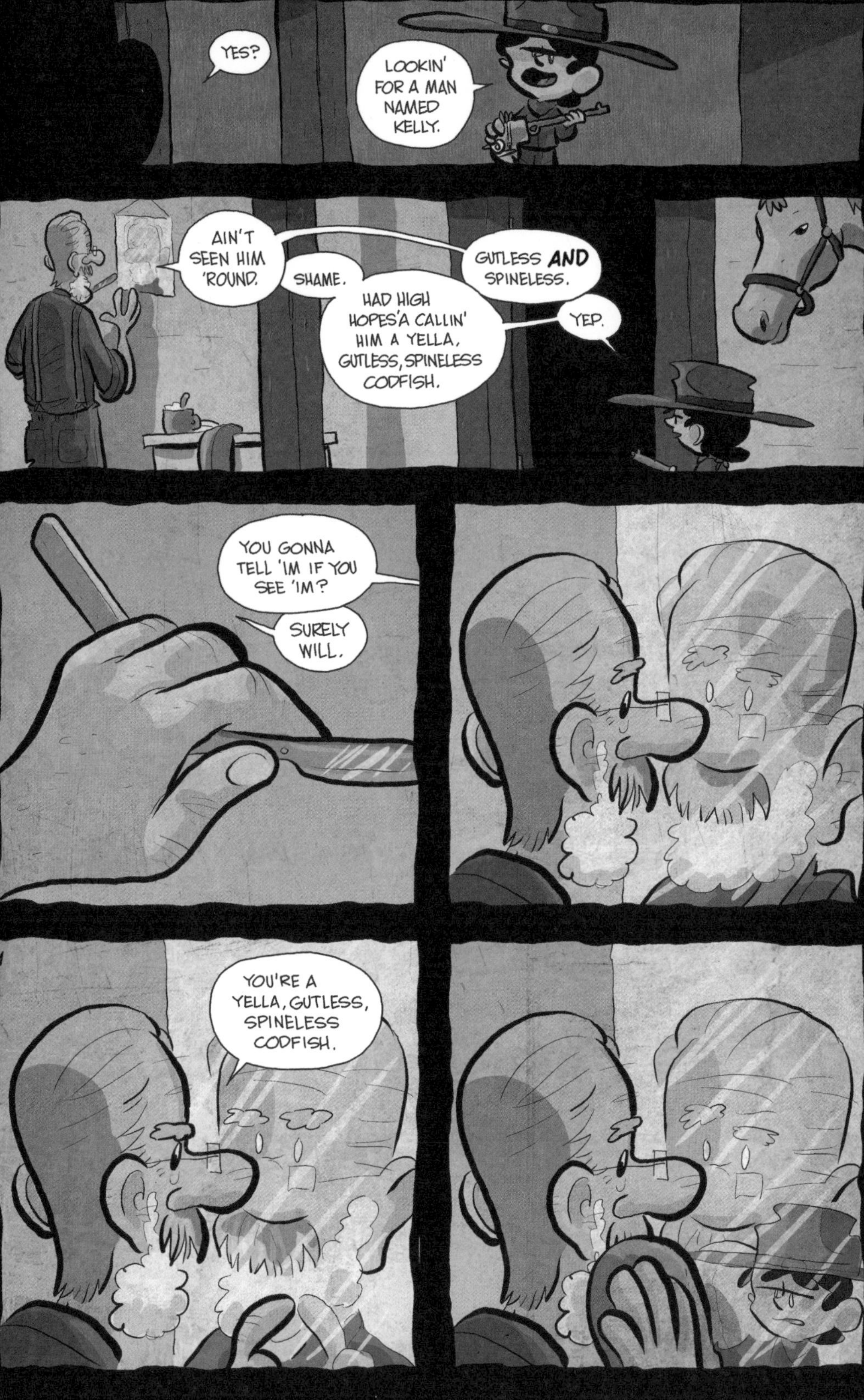
YES?
LOOKIN' FOR A MAN NAMED KELLY.
AIN'T SEEN HIM 'ROUND.
GUTLESS AND SPINELESS.
SHAME.
HAD HIGH HOPES'A CALLIN' HIM A YELLA, GUTLESS, SPINELESS CODFISH.
YEP.
YOU GONNA TELL 'IM IF YOU SEE 'IM?
SURELY WILL.
YOU'RE A YELLA, GUTLESS, SPINELESS CODFISH.

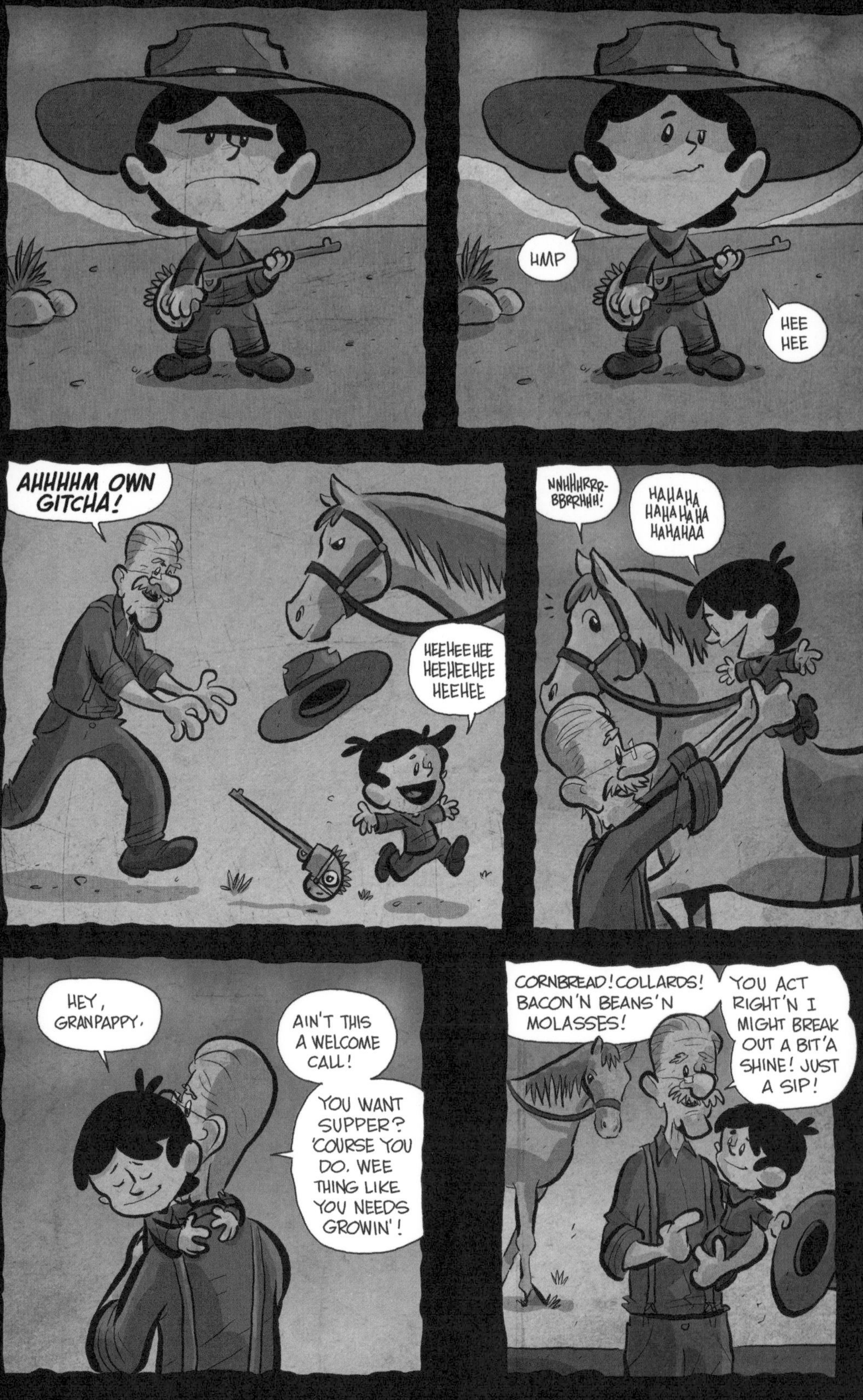

HMP
HEE HEE
AHHHHM OWN GITCHA!
HEEHEEHEE HEEHEEHEE HEEHEE
NNHHHRRR-BBRRHHH!
HAHAHA HAHAHAHAHA HAHAHAA
HEY, GRANPAPPY.
AIN'T THIS A WELCOME CALL!
YOU WANT SUPPER? 'COURSE YOU DO. WEE THING LIKE YOU NEEDS GROWIN'!
CORNBREAD! COLLARDS! BACON'N BEANS'N MOLASSES!
YOU ACT RIGHT'N I MIGHT BREAK OUT A BIT'A SHINE! JUST A SIP!

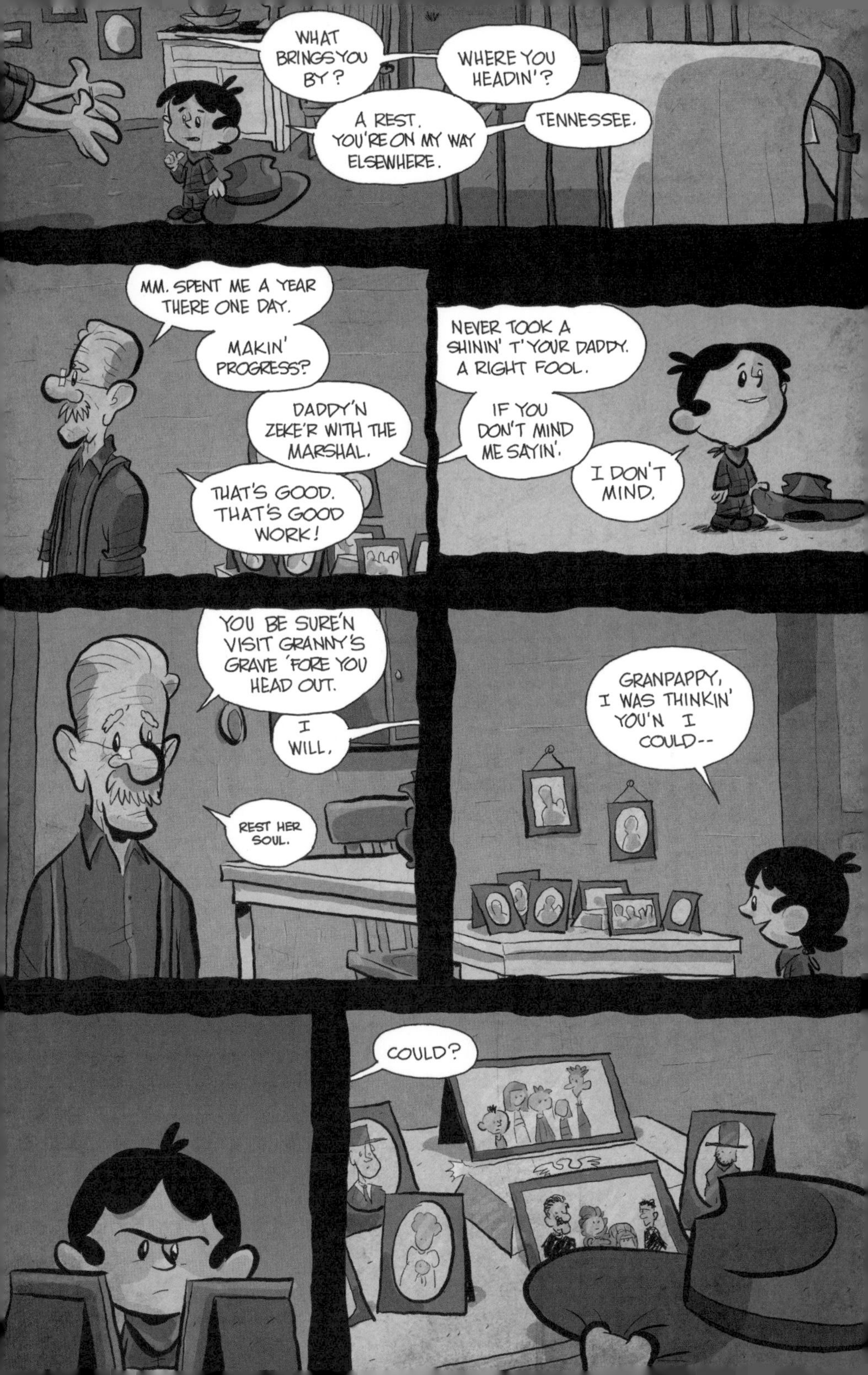
WHAT BRINGS YOU BY?
WHERE YOU HEADIN'?
A REST. YOU'RE ON MY WAY ELSEWHERE.
TENNESSEE.
MM. SPENT ME A YEAR THERE ONE DAY.
MAKIN' PROGRESS?
DADDY'N ZEKE'R WITH THE MARSHAL.
THAT'S GOOD. THAT'S GOOD WORK!
NEVER TOOK A SHININ' T'YOUR DADDY. A RIGHT FOOL.
IF YOU DON'T MIND ME SAYIN'.
I DON'T MIND.
YOU BE SURE'N VISIT GRANNY'S GRAVE 'FORE YOU HEAD OUT.
I WILL.
REST HER SOUL.
GRANPAPPY, I WAS THINKIN' YOU'N I COULD--
COULD?

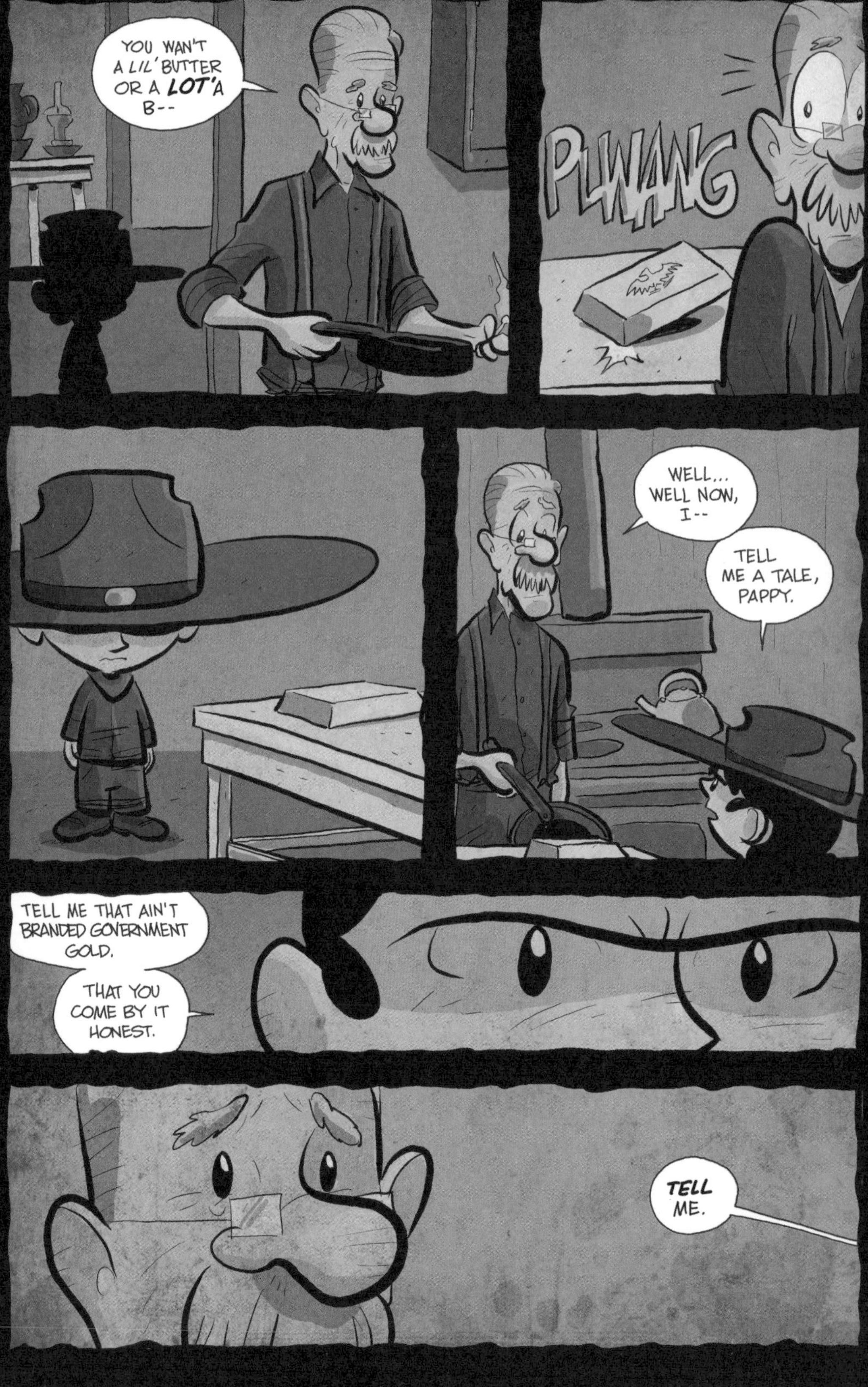
YOU WAN'T A LIL' BUTTER OR A LOT'A B--
PLWANG
WELL... WELL NOW, I--
TELL ME A TALE, PAPPY.
TELL ME THAT AIN'T BRANDED GOVERNMENT GOLD.
THAT YOU COME BY IT HONEST.
TELL ME.

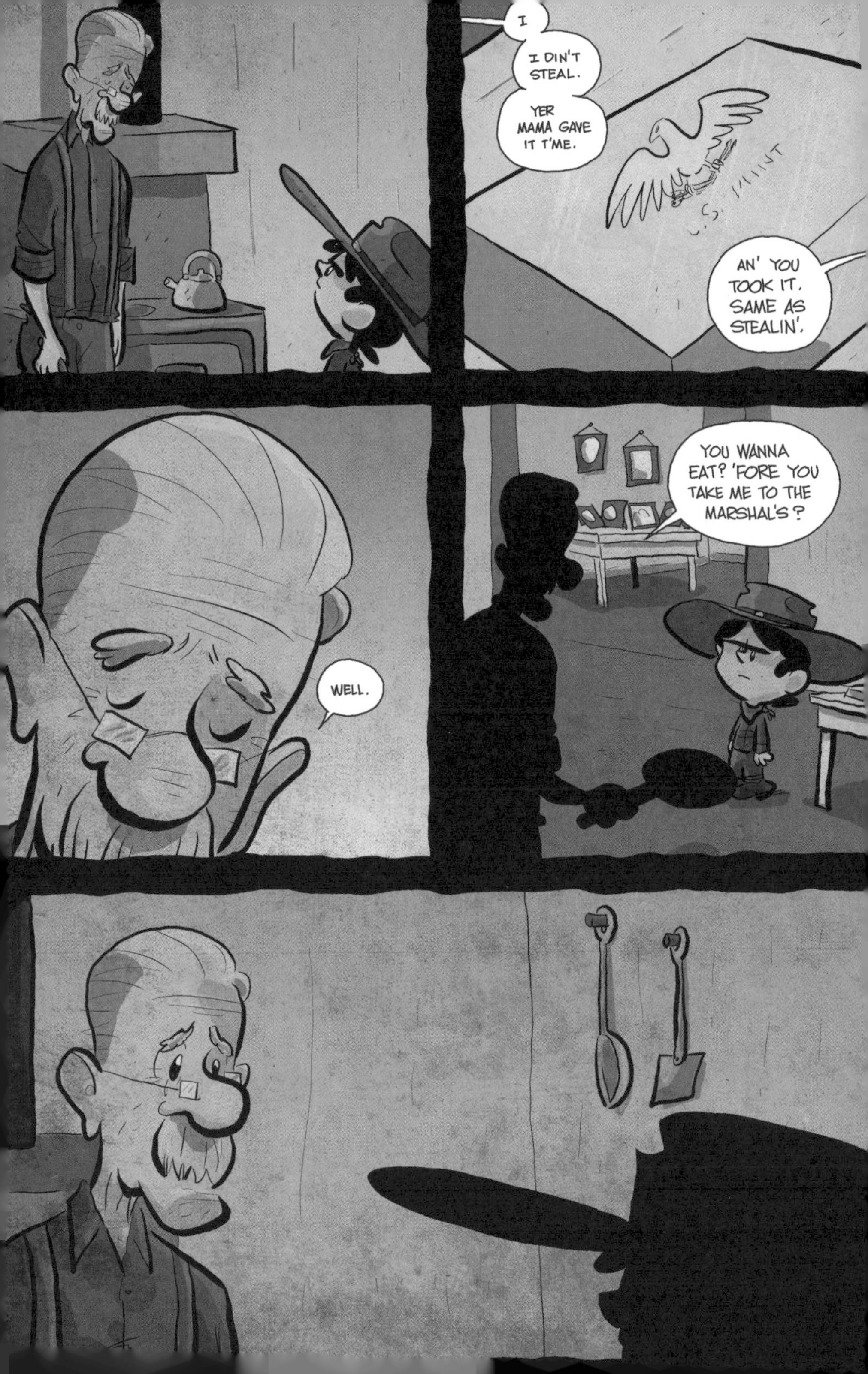
I
I DIN'T STEAL.
YER MAMA GAVE IT T'ME.
AN' YOU TOOK IT. SAME AS STEALIN'.
WELL.
YOU WANNA EAT? 'FORE YOU TAKE ME TO THE MARSHAL'S?

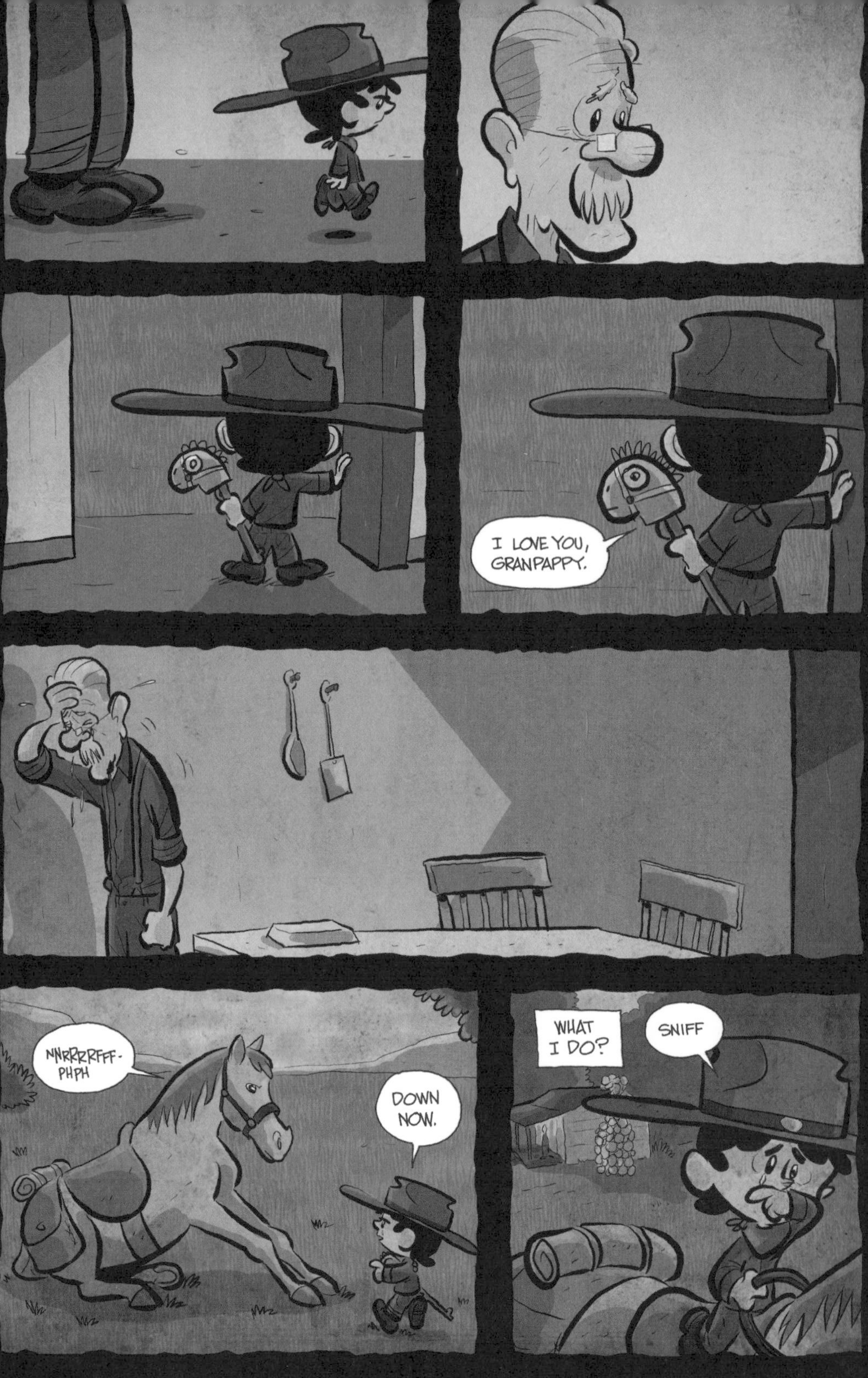
I LOVE YOU, GRANPAPPY.
NNRRRRFFF-PHPH
DOWN NOW.
WHAT I DO?
SNIFF

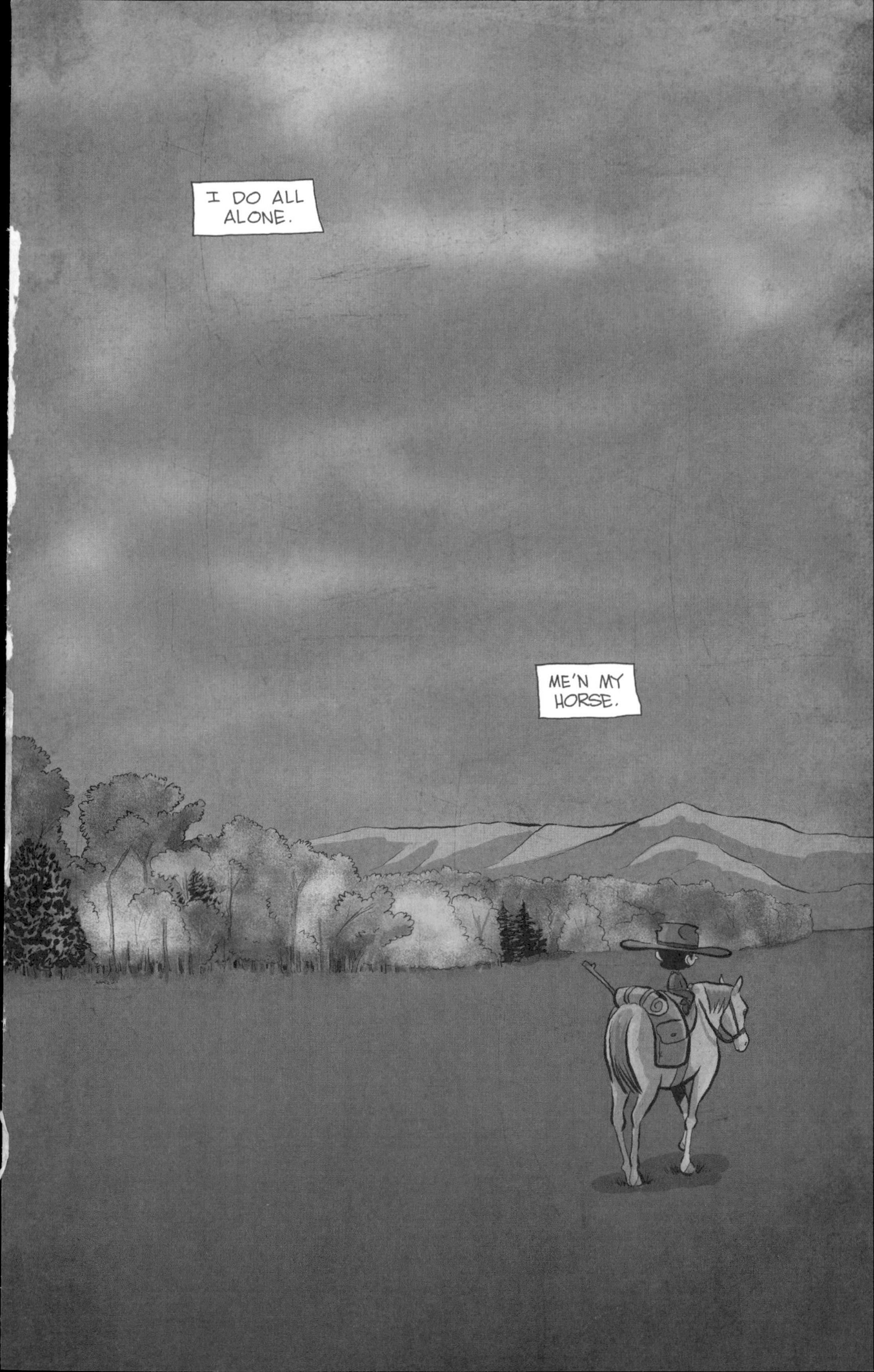
I DO ALL ALONE.
ME'N MY HORSE.

NATE COSBY

was born in Memphis and raised in Mississippi. He was an editor at Marvel Entertainment for six years, overseeing acclaimed series including the Harvey Award-winning Thor The Mighty Avenger, the Eisner Award-winning Wonderful Wizard of Oz and Marvelous Land of Oz, as well as X-Men First Class, Spider-Man, Pride & Prejudice, Sense & Sensibility and many others. Nate's been a producer/writer for PBS' relaunched Electric Company, where he developed animated properties (such as Captain Cluck). He edited Immortals: Gods And Heroes and co-wrote/edited Jim Henson's The Storyteller for Archaia Entertainment, and currently writes Buddy Cops for Dark Horse Entertainment and Pigs with Ben McCool for Image Comics.
Follow Nate on Twitter: @NateCosBOOM.

CHRIS ELIOPOULOS

has been telling stories for as long as he can remember. He started in comics as a letterer working on more comics than he can count. (Mostly because he's bad at math) He's also written and drawn the Eisner and Harvey nominated Franklin Richards: Son of a Genius as well as writing the acclaimed series, Lockjaw and the Pet Avengers for Marvel Entertainment. He's also the author of the webcomic, Misery Loves Sherman. He's short and likes to stay home with his lovely wife, Audra, and their awesome sons Jeremy and Justin and he hates writing in the third person.
Follow Chris on Twitter: @ChrisEliopoulos.

BOYD'S WAGON.

A Cow Boy Short Story.

Had me a wagon. Daddy gave it to me.

"Never had me no wagon growin' up!" he told me. "Take care'a that now. Don't go breakin' a wheel off yer first play."

I went off'n played. Didn't break a wheel. When I came back from playin', Daddy was gone. For good this time.

A summer later, I loaded my worldly possessions in that wagon'n left my mama's home under cover of the night sky. For good this time.

As I walked down the road, I came upon a boy a head taller'n me. "Turn that wagon on its side!" he hollered. He kicked it over, knockin' it on its side. On the bottom of the wagon, ADAM was scratched near the front axle.

'I'm Adam," he said, an' pulled out a bowie knife from his coveralls. 'Ah carved mah name there with this."

I wasn't what I am now. He woulda whupped me fierce. I picked the wagon up, put two apples in it, and said "This wagon was given to me by my daddy. But it wasn't his to give. You wanna whup me, I understand. But the wrong I done to you wasn't by intention."

Adam looked at me. He looked at his wagon and the apples. Then he pocketed his knife, grabbed the wagon handle and walked on down the road.

I stood there watchin' Adam til I couldn't see him no more. I put all my possessions in a towel'n slung it over my shoulder, started walkin' the opposite direction.

That was the night I became a bounty hunter. That was the night my kin's fate was sealed.

Justice
ain't got
no age